Distinctives

Distinctives

Dare To Be Different

Vaughan Roberts

Authentic

First published 2000 by OM Publishing
Reprinted 2000, 2001, 2002
Reprinted 2003 by Authentic Lifestyle

15 14 13 12 11 10 09   15 14 13 12 11 10 9

Reprinted 2005, 2006, 2007, 2009, 2011 by Authentic Media Limited
52 Presley Way, Crownhill, Milton Keynes, MK8 0ES
www.authenticmedia.co.uk

British Library Cataloguing in Publication Data

A catalogue record for this book is available from the
British Library

ISBN 9781-85078-331-2

Cover design by Emily Travers
Printed and bound by CPI Group (UK) Ltd., Croydon, CR0 4YY

To Ben, Tom, Edward, Olivia, James and Jacob

Contents

Acknowledgements

I am grateful to James Dudley-Smith, Clare Heath-Whyte and Alistair Horn for commenting on the manuscript, Jay Bruce for suggesting the title, Liz Chang for her typing, Alistair Cory for the illustrations and Tara Smith for preparing the discussion questions.

Introduction

Do not conform any longer to the pattern of this world, but be transformed by the renewing of your mind. (Rom. 12:2)

An experiment was conducted a few years ago to study the effect of peer pressure on young people. The participants were told that their eye sight was being tested. Some cards would be held up featuring three lines: 'A', 'B' and 'C'. The researchers gave the instructions: 'The lines will be of varying lengths. Sometimes "A" will be the longest, sometimes "B", et cetera. We will point to each in turn. Simply raise your hand when we point to the longest line.' Before the experiment began, nine of the teenagers had been secretly told that they should vote for the second longest line. What would the tenth do? The researchers held up the cards. 'C' was clearly longer than the others, but nine hands went up immediately when a finger pointed to 'B'. The tenth young man, the one being studied, looked confused. He later explained what he had been thinking: 'Perhaps I didn't listen properly to the instructions. I had better do the same as everyone else or they will laugh at me.' So, after a moment, he raised his hand along with the rest of

them. Before repeating the test, the instructions were underlined: 'Raise your hand when we point to the *longest* line.' Then a second card was held up. Once more, nine people voted for the wrong line. This time the poor teenager hesitated for longer, but eventually his hand went up with the group. He did the same thing over and over again – even though he knew that the others were wrong. He was not alone – far from it. More than 75 per cent of young people tested behaved in the same way. They preferred to say that a short line was longer than a long line rather than stand out from the crowd. It was more important to them to fit in than to be right.[1]

It is not just teenagers who are affected by peer pressure. A conformist instinct lies deep within most of us. No wonder we find the Christian life so hard, for Christ calls us to be distinct from those around us. That is the theme of this book. It has been written for those who have already put their trust in Christ. We cannot earn his friendship by living good lives. The only way to be accepted into God's family is to rely not on what we do but on what Christ did for us when he died in our place on the cross. He has done everything necessary. But, as the old saying goes, if we are not saved *by* good works, we are saved *for* good works. The Lord Jesus expects his forgiven people to be different from others. Each chapter focuses on an area in which the demands of God's kingdom are radically different from the norms of our culture. Too often we let ourselves be moulded by others, but Christ longs to use *us* to change *them*. Paul urged the Christians at Rome: 'Do not conform any longer to the pattern of this world, but be transformed by the renewing of your mind.' Will we take up the challenge? Will we dare to be different?

Notes

[1] James Dobson, *Preparing for Adolescence* (Regal, 1989), 45–7.

1

Perspective in a World that Lives for the Moment

For the grace of God that brings salvation has appeared to all men. It teaches us to say "No" to ungodliness and worldly passions, and to live self-controlled, upright and godly lives in this present age, while we wait for the blessed hope – the glorious appearing of our great God and Saviour, Jesus Christ, who gave himself for us to redeem us from all wickedness and to purify for himself a people that are his very own, eager to do what is good. (Tit. 2:11–14)

It was our first time up Snowdon in North Wales and my sister was scared – really scared. We were approaching a cliff that offered some spectacular views, but they were lost on her. She insisted on fixing her gaze on the ground immediately in front of her and refused to look up. If she had looked backwards, she would have been reassured by the sight of solid ground. And if she had looked ahead, she would have been able to see the danger and make sure she avoided it, but none of us could persuade her to do anything but stare straight down. She was reduced to a pathetic shuffle, which must have limited the enjoyment of the walk and certainly increased the danger.

The picture of my sister on that mountain is a picture of modern humanity. Our gaze is fixed downwards – on this present world. Hardly, if ever, do we look back to where we have come from, or forward to where we are going. Our vision is limited to the present, at the expense of the past and the future. This preoccupation with 'the here and now' is a legacy of the scientific age.

There is a fascinating dialogue in one of the 'X Files' episodes. Mulder asks, 'When science can't offer an explanation, can't we turn to the fantastic?' Scully, ever the sceptic, replies, 'What I find fantastic is any notion that there is anything beyond science.' Scully represents what might be called 'scientific fundamentalism' – the belief that nothing exists beyond what can be proved by strict scientific method. That mindset is dominated by the material world – what can be seen, touched and examined. It dismisses anything else as mere fantasy. We can know nothing, we are told, of what happened before this world came into being; or of what, if anything, exists beyond it.

Stephen Hawking is one of the most brilliant physicists and cosmologists of our generation. His book, *A Brief History of Time*, adorns countless coffee tables all over the world. If you want to embarrass those who own the book, just ask them if they have read it. In his conclusion, Hawking laments the unsatisfying nature of science:

> Even if there is only one possible unified theory, it is just a set of rules and equations. What is it that breathes fire into the equations and makes a universe for them to describe? The usual scientific approach of science of constructing a mathematical model cannot answer the question of why there should be a universe for the model to describe. Why does the universe go to all the bother of existing?[1]

Science cannot answer that question – it lies beyond this present world.

If science is silent on that fundamental issue of our past, neither does it have anything to say about our most pressing concern in the future. Throughout history, human beings have wanted to know what happens after death. All science can do is examine the dead body that remains, but that is where it must stop. The world to come is beyond the scope of scientific investigation – it cannot be placed under a microscope. No surgeon has ever discovered a soul. Many conclude, therefore, that there is nothing beyond this world. Bertrand Russell spoke for many when he said, 'When I die I rot.' Another man had these words inscribed on his grave: 'This is the absolute end.' Others find it depressing to dismiss all thoughts of an afterlife, so they cling to some vague belief in the hereafter – but it since this theory has no influence on their behaviour, its role is simply to provide comfort when it is needed.

The scientific age has produced a society which walks through life with its gaze fixed downwards. Robbed of its past and its future, it focuses almost entirely on the present. 'Live for the moment' is the message the media shouts at us. The slogan of a beer commercial is typical: 'You only go round once in life, so grab for all the gusto you can get'.[2] Just the other day I watched a programme on television which featured a man who took those words seriously. He was sitting by the swimming pool of his newly acquired villa in Spain, sipping an exotic drink, and he said: 'I don't really believe that there is anything beyond what we've got here, so I had better enjoy it to the full now.' Such thinking has even invaded the religious world. One American preacher was recently criticized for his extravagance. He replied: 'What's the big deal for goodness sake? What am I supposed to drive – a Honda? ... I am sick and tired of hearing about streets of gold. I don't need gold in heaven – I've got to have it now.' [3]

As Christians we are called to be different. If we walk with our heads down, with our attention fixed entirely on this present world, then we will be 'worldly' Christians. We will be just the same as everyone around us. Each chapter of this book will present us with a choice. Will we live simply for the present, or will we live in the light of God's unseen realities, which science could can never discover on its own? The Bible gives us perspective. Our vision as Christians is not limited to the present. God has revealed truth to us about the past and the future and we are to live now in the light of these truths. If we are to go God's way, we must look beyond 'the here and now' and make sure we are constantly looking both forwards and backwards. That is what the apostle Paul is urging us to do in Titus 2:11–14.

A high standard

Titus was a colleague of Paul's who had been left on the Mediterranean island of Crete to disciple some new converts. Paul wrote to give him instructions about what to teach them. Chapter 2 of Paul's letter to Titus focuses on the need to live a godly life. Its instructions are as relevant to us today as they were to the young Christians on Crete. They set a high standard.

Paul urges us 'to say "No" to ungodliness and worldly passions' (Tit. 2:12). That word 'no' can be one of the hardest in the English language to say, especially if there are voices all around us urging us to say the opposite. Think of the temptations with which you struggle most frequently. There is a powerful triumvirate conspiring to make you give in to them – what some have called 'the evil Trinity'. The world (non-Christian society and friends) tells us: 'Go on, everyone does it. Do you really want to be the odd one out all the time?' Our sinful nature (what the older versions of the Bible used to call 'the flesh') also joins in: 'Why don't you do what you want for a change? It won't do any harm. You only live once – why miss out on all the pleasures of life? God will understand. Anyway, it's only natural.' And behind both those appeals stands the third force, the devil – the malevolent promoter of all the evil in the world. It will not be easy to say 'no' to what is wrong in the face of such powerful forces. Did you notice how the focus of all three is entirely on the present? They try to keep our gaze fixed on the immediate – the fleeting pleasures of sin and the demands to conform to peer pressure.

The high standard Paul sets is not simply negative. There is more to Christian discipleship than avoiding what is wrong. We are also called 'to live self-controlled, upright and godly lives in this present age' (v. 12). Too often we Christians are known in our social groups only for what we do not do ('he doesn't swear, get drunk or sleep around'). It would be wonderful if our friends also went on to comment on our positive qualities: 'She's always got a kind word about everyone and she goes out of her way to help others ...' But it will not be easy to stand out like that. Once again we will experience the opposition of 'the world, the flesh and the devil' seeking to prevent us from going God's way. As before, their voices urge us to keep our eyes fixed downwards on this present world: 'Why go to all the effort of putting yourself out for others? What's in it for you? It's much easier just to go with the flow. Do you really want to be known as one of those "God Squadders"?'

Moral instruction alone will not be enough to ensure that we resist the pressure to conform and instead live a godly life. I know that from my own experience. I worked out recently that I had attended about twenty-five hundred religious services before I became a Christian – that is a lot of religion. I went to church regularly with my parents and attended chapel at school. In sermon after sermon I was exhorted to be a good citizen, to love my neighbour and to avoid what were enigmatically called 'the sins of the flesh'. Those sermons had no impact on me, except to induce occasional feelings of guilt. Why should I bother to live like that? What was in it for me? As far as I could tell, following Christian morality promised to reduce both my enjoyment of life and my image among my friends. I concluded that it would not be worth the effort.

There was very little wrong with what I was taught in all those services – it was, for the most part, authentic Christian morality. The problem was what was not taught – there was no gospel. Christian morality without the Christian gospel is like a car without an engine – there is no power in it. The standards which were set seemed quite unrealistic for an averagely sinful school-boy like myself. I had to wait a long time, but eventually someone explained to me the good news about what Christ had done. For the first time I found I wanted to live the Christian life. There was a joy, a purpose, a passion that I had never had before – at last the engine was in place. I was no longer going through life with my head fixed downwards. My gaze had been lifted up – and that made all the difference.

The gospel gave me perspective. As long as I focused simply on the present, there seemed little point in living according to Christian standards. With my limited vision I could only see the problems – the reaction of my friends and the things I would have to give up. But the good news about Jesus stopped me from staring down-wards and pointed me forwards and backwards as well. I found that what God revealed about the past and the future gave me all the incentives I needed at least to try to live the Christian life.

It is not easy living God's way – saying 'no' to what is evil and 'yes' to what is good. If we are to find the moti-vation to begin to live as he wants, we must fix our attention on the good news about Jesus. That is where this passage in Titus chapter 2 points us. The Bible never divorces morality from the gospel, as the preachers I heard as a boy did. Morality and the gospel belong together. Having spelt out the standards of Christian behaviour in the present (which is the focus of vv. 1–10 as well as v. 12), Paul reminds us of the gospel with its focus on the past and the future. He is giving us the motivation we need to obey the standard he has set. We are to live in 'this present age' in the light of what God has done and will do in history. In particular, we are reminded here of two great appearances of Christ – in the past and in the future.

The appearance of Christ in the past

If this present world is all there is, as the likes of Scully from the 'X Files' will tell us, there is little incentive to make the effort to stand out and be different from everyone else. But her narrow form of scientific reductionism generates a blinkered view of the world. We are not limited to staring downwards at this present world all the time. The Lord Jesus has made it possible for us to look up – to glimpse an unseen world beyond. He came from outside time and space to bear witness to another realm – the kingdom of God. Paul refers to his Christ's coming in verse 11: 'The grace of God that brings salvation has appeared to all men'. It is the good news of that appearance which enables us to do something that would be impossible otherwise: 'It teaches us to say "No" to ungodliness and worldly passions, and to live self-controlled, upright and godly lives.'

It is striking that we have to be 'taught' to live godly lives. The battle of temptation is won and lost in the mind. A persistent appeal to the will to be godly will bear little fruit. It is not enough simply to be told, 'pull your socks up'. The will needs to be educated before it will make an effort. It is as we are pointed back to the great truths concerning what Christ has done for us in history that we will begin to want to please him. Paul knew that, which is why he follows his moral instructions in Titus 2:1–10 with a reminder of the gospel in verses 11 to 14. Our hearts would have to be very hard indeed to not be stirred to obedience by what he writes.

The Lord Jesus did not simply come to earth to reveal God to us – he came to rescue us. Paul reminds us that he 'gave himself for us to redeem us from all wickedness' (v. 14). Jesus did not have to die. The Roman authorities did only what he allowed them to do. His life was not so much taken from him as it was given up for us. Jesus gave himself in an act of self-sacrificial love. A soldier in the First World War was badly wounded in the trenches. As he lay in hospital a doctor had to give him some bad news: 'I'm sorry – you've lost your arm.' The soldier replied, 'I didn't lose it. I gave it.'⁴ In a similar way, Jesus did not simply lose his life – he gave it. There could be no greater gift. And it had a purpose – to 'redeem' us. Without Christ, our situation was helpless, but he has set us free.

It is very easy to catch a monkey. You simply have to make a hole in a coconut shell and put a pebble inside. The monkey is attracted by the pebble and puts its hand into the shell to grab hold of it. Once his hand is inside, it is trapped – its clenched fist is too large to get out. Escape is very easy in theory – the monkey just has to let go and its hand will fit through the hole again. But that is easier said than done. Having got the pebble, the monkey is very reluctant to lose it, so it sits there helpless until its captor arrives. It is trapped by its own desire. We humans are similar. We cannot stop ourselves from clutching what is wrong. The result is that we are unable to escape the inevitable consequence of our wrongdoing, the judgement of God. But, in his great love, God the Father sent his son Jesus to set us free. To 'redeem' means to set free by the payment of a price. That price was the death of Jesus in our place. He died to take the punishment that we deserved so that we need no longer face it.

But there was a further reason for Christ's death. He
died for us both to 'redeem us from all wickedness' and
also 'to purify for himself a people who are his very
own, eager to do what is good' (v. 14). We have been set
free from the tyranny of our old master so that we can
belong to a new one – the Lord Jesus himself. As
Christians we are his people. He has called us to himself
for a purpose – that we might live godly lives. His death
did not simply rescue us from evil; it was designed to set
us apart for what is good. Surely those truths should
provide the incentive we need to resist temptation and
to make the effort to live a different way.

There were two men in a train compartment one day.
One of them fell on the floor and began to have a con-
vulsive fit. His friend knelt down beside him, loosened
his tie and put a handkerchief in his mouth to prevent
him biting his tongue. When the fit had passed, the
friend said to the others in the carriage:

> I'm sorry, but this happens most days. We were in the
> Korean war together. I was injured and left in no-man's
> land. I would have died but my friend came to get me.

He put me over his shoulder and dragged me towards our lines. Just as we were about to get to safety a shell went off. It took a long time for me to get better but eventually I was allowed home to America. I got a good job, met a girl and bought a house – life was going well, but all along I could not stop wondering what had happened to my English friend who had risked his life to save mine. Then I heard that he was like this and would never get better, needing constant care and attention. As soon as I discovered that, I sold my house, gave up my job and broke off my engagement. You see, he did all that for me. There is nothing that I would not do for him.[5]

The Lord Jesus has done even more for us. He gave up his life for us. Surely we should respond by saying: 'He did all that for me, there is nothing I would not do for him.' It is hard to say 'no' to evil and 'yes' to godliness, but it is possible. Temptations focus on the immediate. They point us to things in this world – the allure of some instant pleasure, the attraction of material possessions, the idol of popularity. As long as our eyes are fixed on such things, we will fall every time. But the gospel teaches us to look up to another world – the kingdom of God. When you are next tempted to do something wrong, or tempted to refrain from doing something good, remember the cross. Remind yourself what Jesus did for you. 'He died to set me free from wickedness. How can I go back to it? What appalling ingratitude that would be! Surely the effort involved in living a godly life pales into insignificance compared to what it cost him to die for me.' Do not just think about the present – the fleeting pleasure that sin would give you. The gospel gives us perspective and points us to the past. The appearance of Christ in the past is a powerful incentive to live for him now.

The appearance of Christ in the future

Paul encourages us not just to look back, but to look forward as well. Christians are waiting people: 'We wait for the blessed hope – the glorious appearing of our great God and Saviour Jesus Christ' (v. 13). He has come to this earth in the past and he will come again. That Second Coming will mark the end of 'this present age' and the fulfilment of all God's purposes for his creation. He will undo all the effects of sin and recreate a perfect world for ever. Then at last we will enjoy all the blessings of our salvation. What we have received now is wonderful – forgiveness of sins, friendship with God by the Holy Spirit, Christian fellowship – but most of God's gifts for us as his people await us in the future. And they are guaranteed. Our hope is no fantasy – it is based on the solid reality of the resurrection of Jesus from the dead.

I was once on holiday near Cape Town in South Africa and went on a trip to Seal Island. We were barely out of the harbour when one little seal appeared and swam around our boat. Everyone got very excited. We pushed forward to get the best possible view and all the cameras began to click busily. About half an hour later we reached the island. It was covered with thousands of seals, and the sea was teeming with them. Those of us who had been so excited by the single rather pathetic specimen earlier were rightly embarrassed – especially the poor tourist who had no film left to record the real thing. In a similar way, we Christians will be embarrassed in heaven if we act as if what we have now is all there is. Our eyes should be fixed above all on the future. The Bible makes that point again and again. We are 'aliens and exiles' who do not belong in this world – our citizenship is in heaven. We are to set our minds on 'things above, not on earthly things' (Col. 3:2) and to 'store up for ourselves treasures in heaven' (Mt. 6:20).

Jim Packer presents a devastating critique of western Christianity in his book *Laid-back Religion*. It is, he says:

> ...this-worldly in a way that can only be described as a radical distortion. For today, by and large, Christians no longer live for heaven, and therefore no longer understand, let alone practise, detachment from the world. Nowadays, nonconformity to the world is limited to the means that the world adopts to achieve its goals, and rarely touches the goals themselves. Does the world around us seek pleasure, profit and privilege? So do we. We have no readiness or strength to renounce these objectives, for we have recast Christianity into a mould that stresses happiness above holiness, blessings here above blessings hereafter, health and wealth as God's best gifts, and death, especially early death, not as thankworthy deliverance from the miseries of a sinful world, but as the supreme disaster.... Is our Christianity out of shape? Yes, it is, and the basic reason is that we have lost the New Testament's two-world perspective that views the next life as more important than this one and understands life here as essentially preparation and training for life hereafter.[6]

Packer is surely right. Our Christianity has become 'this-worldly'. No wonder there is often little difference between those inside and those outside the church. If we are to live distinctive lives it is vital that we change our orientation from the present to the future. Why bother to live the Christian life if this world is all there is? I might as well 'live for the moment' along with everyone else – 'if it feels good, do it'. The question of whether I will live for this world or the next underlies every chapter of this book. Without heaven I might as well join the material-istic striving for possessions – there would be nothing to enjoy in the future so I would be foolish not to try to get all I can now. And there would be no point in standing for truth. Why tell others about Jesus when that will offend people in a relativistic world? If there is nothing beyond the grave, there is no urgency in evangelism. In fact, there is no urgency in serving Christ at all.

But there *is* a heaven, and a hell. Jesus *is* coming again. When he comes we will all have to stand before him, our judge. Those who have trusted in Christ will go to be with him in his new creation for ever. The rest will face the awful punishment of separation from him. Christian believers have nothing to fear – Christ has taken our punishment already. But there is no room for compla-cency. We will have to give an account to him as to how we have lived our lives.[7] Will that be an occasion of joy or shame? We belong to the perfect world that will come into being at the end of time and we are called to live now according to its standards. It is not that sin is impossible for us – that, sadly, is far from true. Rather, sin is inappropriate for us. Sin will have no part in the new world for which Christ has rescued us and, in the light of our future, we are to make every effort to root it out of our present lives.

My sister was severely limited in her journey up Snowdon by her insistence on looking straight down at the ground in front of her. Our society is hindered in a similar way. We live in a world which has its eyes fixed downwards and lives only for the present. The gospel points us away from the here and now to consider both the past and the future. Perhaps we should develop a Christian green cross highway safety code. Every child knows the importance of the mantra, 'Look right, look left, look right again.' We should be saying something similar to ourselves: 'Look up, look back, look forward.' Too many of our attitudes and decisions are based on the perspective of this present world alone. We spend too much of our time looking down. We need regularly to remind ourselves regularly to 'Look up, look back, look forward.' 'Look up' to God and the reality of his existence. 'Look back' to what he has done in history through his Son and his death on the cross. 'Look forward' to his coming again and the new eternal world that he will introduce. Those hidden realities will give us the perspective we need to 'dare to be different' and to live distinctive lives. They underlie all the chapters that follow.

Discussion questions

1. What factors have made us a society fixed on the present? What are the implications of 'living for the moment'?
2. How does the gospel give perspective?
3. Why did Christ die for us?

For personal reflection.
How would your perspective change if you were to consciously 'look up, look back, look forward'? What are some of your attitudes that are based on the perspective of this present world alone?

Notes

[1] Stephen Hawking, *A Brief History of Time* (Bantam Press, 10th anniversary edn, 1998), 209.
[2] R.C. Sproul, *Life Views* (Fleming H. Revell, 1986).
[3] *Sword & Trowel* 3 (1992).
[4] Quoted in Roy Clements, *Introducing Jesus* (Kingsway, 1986), 105.

[5] Ian Barclay, *The Facts of the Matter* (Falcon Books, 1971), 33–4.

[6] J.I. Packer, *Laid-back Religion: A Penetrating Look at Christianity Today* (IVP, 1987), 62–3.

[7] See 1 Cor. 3:12–15; 2 Cor. 5:10.

2

Service in a World
that Looks after Number One

They were on their way up to Jerusalem, with Jesus leading the way, and the disciples were astonished, while those who followed were afraid. Again he took the Twelve aside and told them what was going to happen to him. "We are going up to Jerusalem," he said, "and the Son of Man will be betrayed to the chief priests and teachers of the law. They will condemn him to death and will hand him over to the Gentiles, who will mock him and spit on him, flog him and kill him. Three days later he will rise."

Then James and John, the sons of Zebedee, came to him. "Teacher," they said, "We want you to do for us whatever we ask."

"What do you want me to do for you?" he asked.

They replied, "Let one of us sit at your right and the other at your left in your glory."

"You don't know what you are asking," Jesus said. "Can you drink the cup I drink and or be baptised with the baptism I am baptised with?"

"We can," they answered.

> *Jesus said to them, "You will drink the cup I drink and be baptised with the baptism I am baptised with, but to sit at my right or left is not for me to grant. These places belong to those for whom they have been prepared."*
>
> *When the ten heard about this, they became indignant with James and John. Jesus called them together and said, "You know that those who are regarded as rulers of the Gentiles lord it over them, and their high officials exercise authority over them. Not so with you. Instead, whoever wants to be become great among you must be your servant, and whoever wants to be first must be slave of all. For even the Son of Man did not come to be served, but to serve, and to give his life as a ransom for many."* (Mk. 10:32–45)

Gloria Gaynor had a number one hit in 1979 with her song 'I will survive'. It has been popular ever since with and many have adopted it as their personal anthem. Few songs are chosen more frequently on karaoke nights – or sung so badly.

Isolated individuals

In the past, many people had a strong sense of corporate identity – of belonging to a family, local community or nation. But now, increasingly, we see ourselves not so much as members of a group but as isolated individuals. That is hardly surprising when one considers the social changes that have occurred in recent decades. Ours is a mobile society. Young people today are unlikely to spend all their lives in one town or village like many of their ancestors did. Neighbours come and go with a frequency that discourages any great investment in relationships with them. And the chances are that they work miles from where they live anyway, so we hardly see them.

Friendships in the workplace seldom go much deeper. The days when employees could expect to spend all their working life lives with one company are gone. We are just getting to know one group of colleagues when we, or they, change jobs. The result is an ever-growing phone book full of acquaintances, but very few real friends. Technology offers to fill the gap, but we struggle to get beyond the superficial on the internet and mobile phones. The socialite Tara Palmer-Tomkinson told *Hello* magazine recently that she receives 35 messages on her voice mail every day. But she added, 'I'm still very lonely. I just want one call from someone I really want to hear from.'

The greatest cause of the pervading sense of isolation is the breakdown of family life. I was brought up watching Robert Robinson's 'Ask the Family' on television. Mother, father and two children would take on another family in a general knowledge quiz. Such traditional 'nuclear' households are less common these days – so much so that the BBC had to rewrite the rules of the show when it tried to revive it, because it could not find enough contestants. Under the new rules uncles, aunts, grandparents and same-sex partners are allowed to stand in for absent parents. When the programme was first broadcast in the 1960s only eight per cent of families were headed by single parents. By 1996 that proportion had risen to 21 per cent.[1] Over half of those born since 1960 have come from broken homes, with more than one in three marriages ending in divorce.

The atomized self

In an age of changing, insecure relationships, the only constant is the self – what has been called 'the atomized self'. We are on our own now – the individual against the world. Egocentricity used to be condemned, but now it is commended as essential for survival. 'You've got to look after number 1' – no-one else will. 'I will survive.' The great buzz words of the day are 'self-fulfilment', 'self-worth', 'self-esteem'. The bookshops are full of it. 'Self-help' books are constantly among the best-sellers. They urge us to forget others and look instead to the power within to get us through life's problems. These words from one such book are typical:

> We can cherish ourselves and our lives. We can nurture ourselves and love ourselves. We can accept our won-derful selves, with all our faults, foibles, strong points, weak points, feelings, thoughts and everything else. It's the best thing we've got going for us. It's who we are and who we were meant to be. And it's not a mistake. We are the greatest thing that will ever happen to us. Believe it. It makes life much easier.[2]

Another self-help writer has commented: 'The central value is to be true to oneself. What counts is to follow your star, wherever it leads … People are called to authenticity, it is a vocation. It has become the crucial moral orthodoxy of our time.'[3] Above all, 'be yourself'. No one else should be allowed to get in the way of the happiness we deserve – it is our right. One author has listed 37 rights that we should all enjoy. Among them are the following:

• I have a right to dignity and respect.
• I have a right to make decisions based on my feelings, my judgment, or any reason I choose.
• I have the right to be happy.[4]

There is nothing fundamentally new in all this. Human beings have always been selfish. Placing the self at the centre of everything is the essence of sin and is as old as Adam and Eve. But perhaps it is more shameless now than in previous generations. The cult of 'selfism' is being vigorously promoted. An advertisement in *Psychology Today* provides a striking example: 'I love me. I am not conceited. I'm just a good friend to myself. And I like to do whatever makes me feel good.'[5]

That is the world we live in – a self-centred world. Once again, we find that Jesus expects his followers to live a different way. We are to be distinct. Jesus calls us to a life of service, putting God and others first whatever the cost. And, as we will see in the passage from Mark's gospel, he does not expect us to do what he has not done himself. He is our perfect model.

A shocking request

The scene is set somewhere in Palestine. Jesus is travelling towards Jerusalem with his disciples. James and John sidle up alongside him and say, 'Teacher, we want you to do for us whatever we ask' (v. 35). Jesus replies, 'What do you want me to do for you?' (v. 36). They respond, 'Let one of us sit at your right and the other at your left in your glory' (v. 37).

Before we condemn them for the arrogance of their request, we need to recognize what spiritual insight it actually revealed. It had taken a while, but they have at last recognized that Jesus is no ordinary man. He is God's Messiah – the saviour promised in the Old Testament who would come to earth to establish God's kingdom and put everything right. The prophets had said that the new messianic age would be introduced at Jerusalem, so there is understandable excitement as the disciples approach the city with Jesus. There is great

faith behind what James and John ask. They are confident that Jesus the carpenter will soon be enthroned as
God's great king, and they want to be alongside him
when it happens. The Jews believed that when the
Messiah was installed as king there would be a magnif-
icent feast. It is likely that the two disciples had that
banquet in mind. They wanted the positions of greatest
honour.

There may have been faith behind the request of
James and John, but they were also motivated by self-
interest. There is something of their attitude in all of us.
Sadly, we do not lose the selfish instinct as soon as we
become believers. We might not put it as bluntly, but so
often our concern is also that Jesus should 'do for us
whatever we ask'. We expect the divine genie to come
running whenever we rub our prayer lamps: 'Yes, master, your wish is my command.' We see our faith is seen
as a means of meeting our needs for, or even our 'rights'
to, happiness and contentment. The rebuke of Jesus in
Mark 10 speaks as much to us as to the first disciples. He
stresses a message which we desperately need to hear.
Authentic Christianity is not marked by self-fulfilment
and self-promotion, but rather by suffering and service.

Following Jesus means suffering

The first eight chapters of Mark's Gospel are dominated
by the question, 'Who is Jesus?' Mark points to a great
deal of evidence which proves that he is the Messiah
and, at last, the disciples get the point. It was Peter who
was the first to acknowledge it: 'You are the Christ'
(8:29). That is the turning point of the book. From that
moment on, the focus is on another question: 'Why did
Jesus come?' The answer is a shocking one – he came to

die. Straight after Peter's confession, Mark tells us that 'Jesus began to teach them that the Son of Man must suffer many things and be rejected by the elders, chief priests and teachers of the law, and that he must be killed and after three days rise again' (8:31). That is the first of three predictions of his suffering that Jesus gives his disciples in this Gospel. Each time he gives one of these prophecies, Mark stresses that the disciples fail to understand what Jesus is saying.

Peter was always the first to speak and he often got it wrong. He suffered from a chronic case of 'foot in mouth disease' – he was the kind of person who only opened his mouth to change feet. He could not accept that the great Messiah would have to suffer, and he 'rebuked' Jesus (8:32). He in turn received one of the strongest rebukes in the whole Bible: 'Get behind me, Satan! You do not have in mind the things of God, but the things of men' (8:33). Jesus recognized not just the voice of the world, but of the devil himself, in what Peter said. It was essential that Jesus suffer and die – he could not enter his glory any other way. Yes, he would be raised, but first he must die to save his people from their sins. Anyone who suggested otherwise was offering a satanic temptation.

But Jesus made it clear that he was not the only one who must suffer: 'If anyone would come after me, he must deny himself and take up his cross and follow me' (8:34). The way of the cross is the path to glory – not just for Jesus, but for his disciples as well: 'Whoever wants to save his life will lose it, but whoever loses his life for me and for the gospel will save it' (8:35). That message took a long time to sink in.

There is another prediction of the cross in Mark 9:31–32. Directly afterwards, the disciples had an argument among themselves about which of them was the greatest (9:33–34). We are meant to notice the contrast. Jesus is prepared to lower himself even to the extent of dying, but the disciples are concerned only to exalt themselves. The same contrast is there in Mark 10 which contains the clearest and most brutal prediction of the cross. Jesus described what his suffering would involve in great detail – 'they will mock him and spit on him, flog him and kill him' (v. 34). That is the model for Christian disciples – we are to walk in Jesus' footsteps. But, once again, the disciples failed to understand that. The request of James and John would be shocking in any context but, coming as it does immediately after Jesus' description of his imminent death, there is an added horror: 'We want you to do for us whatever we ask' (v. 35).

A religion of the world

The religion of James and John is a religion of the world. They wanted a discipleship that would bypass suffering and go straight to glory. But that is not possible. Just as Jesus had to suffer on the cross before he was raised to the right hand of his Father in heaven, so his disciples must endure much hardship before they are raised with him. That is why Jesus responds to them as he does: 'You don't know what you are asking. Can you drink the cup I drink or be baptised with the baptism I am baptised with?' (v. 38). In a number of Old Testament passages, the cup is a symbol of God's wrath. In the Garden of Gethsemane Jesus says, 'Take this cup from me. Yet not what I will, but what you will' (Mk. 14:36). The 'cup' stood for the suffering that he was about to endure on behalf of his people (v. 38). Jesus' 'baptism' is also a reference to his death. It was quite common in those days to use the word 'baptism' to speak of the experience of being overwhelmed with trouble. So, the path to greatness in the kingdom of God will not be an easy one. Jesus is saying, 'If you want to be great in my kingdom, you must be willing to drink the cup of suffering. You must expect to be baptised with suffering and possibly even death.'

James and John were full of bravado – they said straight away, 'Yes, of course, we can do that' (v.39). They did not know what they were saying, but, supernaturally, Jesus knew that they would indeed suffer greatly. That is still the calling of Christians today: to suffer with Christ and for Christ – it is the only way to greatness in the kingdom of God. And yet, so often, we find we are like James and John. We are worldly; we want a Christianity that bypasses suffering and heads straight to glory. We want a Christ who massages our egos and soothes our wounds – not one who will add to our suffering. When we go to church on a Sunday we like to be comforted, not challenged – sent into the week with a warm fuzzy feeling inside and a 'Ready-Brek' glow surrounding us. This is a serious distortion of authentic Christianity. Jesus never promised his followers an easy life; quite the opposite – he called his disciples to take up their crosses (Mk. 8:34). If we are faithful disciples then we will face suffering. Are we ready for that?

'Take up your cross'

What happens when there is an apparent conflict between my comfort and Christ's demands? The modern cult of 'selfism' deifies the self – nothing must be allowed to challenge my right to health and happiness. But we Christians should recognize such talk as nothing short of idolatry. There is only one God and I must obey him wherever he leads and whatever it costs. That will not always be easy – living for Christ can be painful.

The pain for us might come in the area of personal morality. Jesus says, 'If your hand causes you to sin, cut it off' (Mk. 10:43). The world tells us that it does not really matter how we behave as long as we do not cause any serious harm to others. But Jesus comes to us with a very different message. We are to be willing to go through agony to get rid of sin. He is not speaking literally, of course – he is not encouraging actual self-mutilation. But his words leave us in no doubt that we should go to any effort to get rid of wrongdoing in our lives. Are we prepared for the suffering that might be involved in that? For some that has meant ending a precious relationship or friendship. I can think of one man who left his job and faced unemployment because he felt unable to resist the pressure to join in some dishonest practice at work. Others have endured the shame of confessing some secret sin because they acknowledged that they needed help to break its power. Bring to mind the areas of your life in which you know you are disobeying Christ. What do you have to do to get rid of that sin? Are you prepared to do that, however difficult it might be?

Living for Christ might affect our relationship with others. Perhaps you are conscious that if you live a consistent Christian life at home or work or among your social group you may lose some friends. They will not understand why you do not join in with all they do. Most people are quite happy for us to be Christians as long as we do not take it all too seriously. How tempting it is to compromise. We become domesticated – very comfortable to live with, but spineless. Christ challenges us to put him first in all situations, whatever the cost.

In a previous generation, large numbers of young people left the security of this country to take the good news of Christ to other continents. It took months to get there to these places – some died on the way. There were none of the usual Western comforts when they arrived. The standard of living was very low, not to mention the standard of hygiene. In some places, life expectancy was limited to a few years. Would any of us go under such circumstances today? We take it for granted that Christ wants us to enjoy a long, prosperous and comfortable life. We need to heed his words to James and John. 'Can you drink the cup I drink and be baptised with the baptism I am baptised with?' We should expect suffering. But it will not go on for ever. The cross was followed by the resurrection. There is a place at a great banquet waiting for all his followers, but we cannot go straight there. First there is a cup to drink and a baptism to endure.

Following Jesus means service

The other disciples were furious when they heard what James and John had asked for. But theirs was not a righteous anger. They were contaminated with the same poison of selfish ambition – they were concerned that the other two may have stolen a march on them by putting in their request for the best seats first. They all needed to hear the correction of Jesus. He gathered them together and said, 'You know that those who are regarded as rulers of the Gentiles lord it over them, and their high officials exercise authority over them' (v. 42). Perhaps he was thinking of the Roman emperors whose images appeared on coins alongside the words 'he who deserves adoration'.[6] The emperors were surrounded by minions who took care of their every need. There is something very attractive in that.

'I want to be king'

My mother has a number of different ways of embarrassing me. One of the most effective ploys she uses is to tell my friends about my early ambitions in life. I was six at the time. The teacher asked the class to draw a pictures of what we wanted to do when we grew up. Mine featured a large hill with a stick man on top of it with a crown on his head. Underneath I had written, 'When I grow up I want to be king'. I now realise that that was a totally unrealistic dream. I have replaced it with a new goal – to captain England at cricket. Judging by their recent performances I am still in with a chance – but only if the selectors come and watch the Cassington village team.

In one sense we all want to be kings. We like the thought of a world that revolves around us, inhabited by people dedicated to serving us. We envy those tennis stars at Wimbledon. All they have to do is nod their

heads and a ball is thrown to them. A quick word brings a Diet Coke, a towel or a banana. That is what greatness involves as far as most people are concerned. But Jesus turns the values of the world totally upside down. He tells us, 'Not so with you. Instead, whoever wants to be great among you must be your servant, and whoever wants to be first must be slave of all' (vv. 43–44). The great one is the servant, not the one he serves.

It has been suggested that the British make the worst waiters in the world – we are so proud that we hate to serve others. This is very demeaning teaching for us; it will not be easy to humble ourselves and put others first. But, once again, Jesus is not asking us to do something that he has not done himself. He suffered – he drank the cup of God's wrath and was baptized with the baptism of death. He served. Our passage ends with some remarkable words: 'Even the Son of Man did not come to be served, but to serve, and to give his life as a ransom for many' (v. 45).

The King on a cross

When we are tempted to think that we are too important to lower ourselves and put ourselves out for others, we need to remember Jesus. He was 'the Son of Man'. That was his preferred way of speaking of himself. It is a title taken from the prophecy of Daniel in the Old Testament where it stands for a figure of tremendous authority. Daniel has a vision of the end of time and sees one he calls 'the Son of Man' receiving an eternal and universal kingdom: 'He was given authority, glory and sovereign power: all peoples, nations and men of every language worshipped him. His dominion is an everlasting dominion that will not pass away' (Dan. 7:14). There could not be a greater figure and yet, says Jesus, even he 'did not come to be served, but to serve'. The world had never seen a king like him before. He should have had a chariot, a crown of jewels and a glorious throne, but instead he chose a donkey, a crown of thorns and a cross. He gave up his life 'as a ransom for many', dying that others might live. He did not stay on that cross. God raised him to life again and now, as the great king of the universe, he calls on us to follow his example. His self-sacrificial service to others is to be the pattern for our lives.

By nature we resent the demands that others place upon us. 'Why should I bother to spend time with the man next door? True, he is lonely after his recent bereavement, but he has never done anything for me. I don't even like him.' 'Yes, I know they need some volunteers to help with the coffee rota – but there must be someone else who could do it. I have such a busy life that I need to be able to switch off when I come to church. And, anyway, isn't it a waste of my talents? I've done a bit of preaching in my time, you know – that would be a more appropriate role for me.' It is a good job that Jesus did not share such attitudes. He was prepared to die for his enemies. The Lord of the universe went to a cross – what could be less 'appropriate'? Are we prepared to follow his example? Of course we cannot do everything. There are so many people who need help and so many jobs that need doing and we have just one life. But could we do more?

For some, the answer will be 'no'. Your time is filled serving others and the Lord Jesus. If so, his words still bring a strong challenge. What is our attitude to this 'service'? It is very easy to serve ourselves even when we appear to be serving others. We enjoy doing what a friend of mine calls 'the hidden humble jobs in the limelight'. Our chests swell as others spot what we are doing and the word goes round the office, 'He has a such a servant heart'. And we smart in those times when no one sees what we have done or bothers to thank us. We love to see our name on the church notice sheet or, better still, on the notice board outside, where more people can see it. And we are livid when a precious job is taken from us. Mrs Jones has led the Sunday School for years – rather badly, if the truth be told. But no-one dares to ask anyone else to do it – she would be furious; it is her life.

Even our Christian 'service' can become an outlet for 'self-fulfilment', 'self-esteem', 'self-glorification'. But we are called to resist the self-centred instinct which our world promotes and follow instead the one who 'made himself nothing, taking the very nature of a servant' (Phil. 2:7). That will not be easy – suffering and service never are, but they are the path to greatness in the eyes of the only one who really matters. Instead of singing, 'I will survive', we should say, 'I will serve'.

Discussion questions

1. Think about how living in a self-centred world has affected you. If you were completely honest, what would you list as your 'rights' or expectations of what you deserve in life?
2. What does it mean that the way of the cross is the path to glory for Jesus? And for his disciples?

For personal reflection.
In what ways might it be painful for you to deny the idolatry of self – perhaps in the area of personal morality? A relationship? Service?

Notes

[1] The *Sunday Times*, 27–12–98.
[2] Melody Beattie quoted in Michael Scott Horton (ed.), *Power Religion* (Moody Press, 1992), 230.
[3] Brian Appleyard in The *Sunday Times*, 7–2–99.
[4] Charles Whitefield, Healing the Child Within, quoted in Horton, *Power*, 227.
[5] Quoted in John R.W. Stott's *The Cross of Christ* (IVP, 1986), 275.
[6] Stott, Cross, 87.

3

Contentment in a World that Never Has Enough

"Do not store up for yourselves treasures on earth, where moth and rust destroy, and where thieves break in and steal. But store up for yourselves treasures in heaven, where moth and rust do not destroy, and where thieves do not break in and steal. For where your treasure is, there your heart will be also.

"The eye is the lamp of the body. If your eyes are good, your whole body will be full of light. But if your eyes are bad, your whole body will be full of darkness. If then the light within you is darkness, how great is that darkness!

"No-one can serve two masters. Either he will hate the one and love the other, or he will be devoted to the one and despise the other. You cannot serve both God and Money.

"Therefore I tell you, do not worry about your life, what you will eat or drink; or about your body, what you will wear. Is not life more important than clothes? Look at the birds of the air; they do not sow or reap or store away in barns, and yet your heavenly Father feeds them. Are you not much more valuable then they? Who of you by worrying can add a single hour to his life?

"And why do you worry about clothes? See how the lilies of the field grow. They do not labour or spin. Yet I tell you that not even Solomon in all his splendour was dressed like one of these. If that is how God clothes the grass of the field, which is here today and tomorrow is thrown into the fire, will he not much more clothe you, O you of little faith? So do not worry, saying, 'What shall we eat?' or 'What shall we drink?' or 'What shall we wear?' For the pagans run after all these things, and your heavenly Father knows that you need them. But seek first his kingdom and his righteousness, and all these things will be given to you as well. Therefore do not worry about tomorrow, for tomorrow will worry about itself. Each day has enough trouble of its own." (Mt. 6:19–34)

Twelve, 15, 26, 44, 46 and 49: six numbers that made two men very happy on 10 June 1995. Mark Gardiner and Paul Maddison shared the record jackpot prize of £22,590,830. With figures like that available, it is hardly surprising that the lottery has become a national obsession. Not long ago if you asked children about their ambitions for the future, they would probably have told you that they wanted to be pop or sports stars. Nowadays they are just as likely to say that they want to win the lottery – it is the great dream of millions.

The desire to 'get rich quick'

All around us, people want to get rich – preferably as quickly as possible and with the minimum effort. I was struck in a bookshop recently by the number of titles that address this desire. There was *Think and Grow Rich* by Napoleon Hill. It has been through 42 editions and sold over seven million copies. Alongside it was *10 Keys to Prosperity* by Gudrun Kretschmann, which begins with an introductory letter:

> Dear Friends, wouldn't it be a different world if we knew that we could all be prosperous? We have the power to build and shape our lives in the way we choose and desire. Only our minds create scarcity. Choose prosperity in your life. Abundance and prosperity on all levels is possible. These keys will assist you in manifesting a life you really want. You deserve it. Love Gudrun.[1]

Notice the assumption that underlies those words – it was there in all the books I looked at – that wealth is the great goal: 'Whatever you do, you must strive to be rich'. Each author has his own quick and easy formula that ensures, so the claim goes, that we achieve that goal. The cover of one book enthused: 'Mark Fisher, an instant millionaire himself and author of the motivational classic, *The Instant Millionaire*, returns to share more of his simple wisdom that will put you on the path to fortune and happiness…. All is possible for those who discover the magic of having a goal and the power to think big.'[2] It is easy to ridicule such nonsense. Does anyone really believe that the path to a fortune simply involves following one or two trite pieces of folksy advice? Presumably they people do – the books sell in by the thousands. These authors feed on the materialistic desire that pervades our society.

We saw in Chapter 1 how science has produced a world that is focused almost entirely on the present and that lives for the moment. A purely scientific world-view encourages the belief that observable things constitute the only reality. The result is that life becomes a never-ending pursuit of things. Have you noticed that one of the most common complaints about houses is that they do not have enough storage space? We have so many possessions

– most of which we do not need, never use or even see. And yet we keep on buying – whether or not we have the money. Someone once commented: 'We humans are very odd. We buy things we don't need, with money we don't have, to please people we don't like'.

That is the world we live in as Christians, and we know the pressure to conform. We are not immune from the allure of the adverts with their seductive messages. 'You haven't lived until you've driven this car, worn these clothes, visited that location', they tell us. And we hear the voice within urging us 'to keep up with the Joneses'. The teenager has to have that particular brand of trainers to avoid acute embarrassment at school – the cheap alternative simply will not do. Adults are no different. How easy it is to yield to the temptation to buy a bigger house and a faster car than we need, just because it is expected of those of our social status. Perhaps Christians are compromised in this area more than any other. Are we really any different from our non-believing friends in our attitudes to wealth and possessions? We need to face the hard challenge of the Lord Jesus. 'No-one can serve two masters... You cannot serve both God and Money' (v. 24). We will have to make a choice. In this passage from the Sermon on the Mount, Jesus leaves his followers in no doubt as to what their choice should be. He points out the folly of materialism (living for money and possessions) and the wisdom of living a different way.

Materialism does not pay

> *Do not store up for yourselves treasures on earth, where moth and rust destroy, and where thieves break in and steal.* (v. 19)

Jesus is not telling his disciples to renounce all personal possessions, nor is he suggesting that it is sinful to save. The

Bible encourages us to praise our Creator for the good things he has given us and to be wise in the way we use them (1 Tim. 6:17–19). The ant is presented as a model for us in the way in which it stores up food in the summer so that it will be ready for the winter (Prov. 6:6). What is forbidden here is not prudent stewardship but selfish accumulation – what one writer has called 'the foolish fantasy that a person's life consists in the abundance of his possessions; and the materialism which tethers our hearts to the earth'.[3] That is what is meant by 'storing up treasure on earth'. Such behaviour is not simply immoral; it is foolish, for nothing in this world will last. The earth is a place 'where moth and rust destroy and thieves break in and steal.'

That thought is too much for modern humanity, which has invested everything in earthly things. We do all we can to escape from the impermanent reality of our world, and we have been quite successful. We have invented mothballs, rustproof paint and burglar alarms, all of which help to preserve our worldly investments. But even if we were successful in finding material things which could last for ever, we would still have to face the uncomfortable fact that we would not be around for very long to enjoy them. Death laughs at those who invest everything in this present world.

The story is told of a clergyman who was asked at a funeral, 'How much did she leave, vicar?' He replied, 'She left everything – they always do.' As the Bible puts it, 'We brought nothing into the world, and we can take nothing out of it' (1 Tim. 6:7). Bill Gates' personal fortune topped the billion-dollar mark in April 1999. One newspaper worked out that if he stacked his money in dollar bills in a pile under his bed, he would have to parachute sixteen miles down to his bedroom floor.[4] That is a lot of money, but he will not be able to take one cent with him beyond the grave.

The rich fool

Jesus' parable of the rich fool is almost a commentary on his words here in verse 19 (Lk. 12:16–21). A man's land yields a good crop and he says to himself: 'You have plenty of good things laid up for many years. Take life easy; eat, drink and be merry.' But he had taken no account of his death. God says to him: 'You fool! This very night your life will be demanded from you. Then who will get what you have prepared for yourself?' If we were to re-tell this story in today's terms it might go something like this. Here is a man who has 'made it' in the eyes of everyone who knows him. He was a great success at university – he was captain of soccer, had a wide circle of friends and got a good first, (although no-one had ever seen him in a library). He was one of those annoying people who had it all. He landed a top job in the city on graduation and it was not long before he was climbing rapidly up the career ladder. By the age of forty-five he had a flat in the Barbican, a large house in the country and a string of racehorses in training. Here we find him on the terrace of his house in Hampshire. Everything he sees is his – the Mercedes in the drive, the horses in the paddock, the rolling fields. He sighs to himself and says, 'I'm doing pretty well in life – I've got everything I could possibly want. I might as well take early retirement and put my feet up so I can enjoy it all.' But he does not get the chance. There is a sudden pain in his chest and he is dead before they get him to the hospital. His friends thought he was so wise – he had made such a success of his life. But God called him a fool – death had not entered his thinking at all. Jesus ends his parable with these words: 'This is how it will be with anyone who stores up things for himself but is not rich towards God.'

The rich fool's fate is a warning to us all. It is always sad to hear of those who have put their life savings into a bank or company which subsequently collapses. Presumably they would have invested elsewhere if they had been able to foresee the future. It would be the height of folly to invest in a business that you know is heading for certain liquidation. And it is folly also to pour our hearts into the pursuit of earthly things which do not last and which cannot be enjoyed for ever. Such an investment of our lives may provide some short-term returns, but it cannot deliver in the long run. Materialism does not pay in the end.

Materialism does not satisfy

> *The eye is the lamp of the body. If your eyes are good, your whole body will be full of light. But if your eyes are bad, your whole body will be full of darkness.* (vv. 22–23)

If materialism does not pay, neither does it does not satisfy either. That is the implication of what Jesus teaches in these verses. A sighted person walks in the light, whereas a blind person must walk in darkness, with all the problems associated with that. There is a great difference between their quality of life, and it is all caused by one tiny organ. Whether an eye functions properly or not has far-reaching implications. That much is obvious. But we are meant to look beyond the surface of what Jesus is saying here to a metaphorical meaning. In the context, the eye stands for the heart. He has just said, 'where your treasure is, there your heart will be also'. Our hearts follow our treasure, whether that is on earth or in heaven. We have to decide where we will invest our lives, and Jesus wants us to be in no doubt that that decision is of vital importance. If our hearts are focused in the right place and we invest in heaven, then our eye is 'good' and our whole lives are flooded with light. But if, on the other hand, we are materialistic and have our hearts fixed on this world, then our eye is bad and we are 'full of darkness'. That is a sombre thought, but what does it mean?

Jesus is teaching that a materialistic mindset affects the whole personality and has disastrous spiritual consequences. Life is reduced to a never-ending quest for money and the possessions it can buy. The focus is on the body, its needs and comforts, at the expense of the spirit. And things become more important than people. That is seen in its ugliest form in the squabbles that so often break out over an inheritance. Someone dryly observed, 'Where there's a will there's a crowd.' Families are torn apart as brothers and sisters, cousins and aunts, fight over who gets the best share of the heirlooms. Such greed is seen all around us. The legacy of the 'loadsamoney' culture of the later Thatcher years still lingers. The rich strive to get richer. They pamper themselves with more and more useless gadgets and luxurious home comforts, and they are blind to the needs of those less fortunate. 'Blindness' is the right expression. Materialism produces a myopia that is unable to see beyond the next pay cheque and what it will buy.

The goal of the materialistic person is a comfortable and contented life, but it is never achieved. Eric Morecambe was the nation's favourite comedian. He earned a fortune from his work, which would have ensured that he had plenty to live on for a long and prosperous retirement, but he kept on working right to the end of his life. After he had a serious heart attack, a friend of his asked him, 'Why don't you slow down?' He replied, 'I can't – I haven't got enough.' He died on stage shortly afterwards at a comparatively early age.

We have seen great increases in our material prosperity in the last few decades and yet we do not seem to be any happier: quite the opposite, in fact, according to evidence recently presented to the intriguingly intriguingly named 'International Congress of Humour' in Switzerland. The average man apparently laughed for 18 minutes per day in the 1950s, compared to only six minutes per day in 1990 – despite vast improvements in the standard of living. The report in my newspaper did not tell me how they came to those figures. Two experts were quoted. A psychologist said:

> The consensus among psychiatrists is that we are now anything up to ten times more likely to be depressed then we were in the Fifties. Advanced consumer capitalism exploits our instincts to compare ourselves to each other vastly more than we used to. We become deeply dissatisfied, relative to others, despite being richer.

Michael Argyle, introduced as 'an expert on happiness', added: 'Those who value money most are less satisfied and in poorer mental health. This may be because money provides only superficial kinds of satisfaction'.[5]

Jesus could have told him that years earlier. It is not just the materialist's treasure that corrodes; his heart does, too. His warped ambitions in life give him a 'bad eye' which darkens his whole personality. The relentless pursuit of possessions makes us greedy, selfish and dissatisfied. An increasing number of people recognize the futility of such an existence. Fenn Chapman, a sixteen-year-old, hit the headlines when he ran away from Rugby School a year or two ago and flew to the Bahamas. He raised the fare by selling his stereo and his collection of CDs. The reporters tracked him down and asked him why he did it. He replied, 'I started thinking about my future: university, a job, buying a car, getting married, a mortgage and then dying. I thought there had to be something more than this. So I had to get away and think things through.'[6] He had recognized the truth of what we have learnt from Jesus: materialism does not pay and does not satisfy. But is there any alternative? If this world is all there is, then we have no choice but to invest our lives in earthly treasures. Jesus insists that there is another, better way to live, made possible because of two hidden realities – a guaranteed future and a generous Father.

A guaranteed future

> *Store up for yourselves treasures in heaven, where moth and rust do not destroy, and where thieves do not break in and steal.* (v. 20)

'Treasures on earth' will not last, but 'treasures in heaven' are eternally secure. Because Jesus died and rose again, all who trust in him have a guaranteed future – what the apostle Peter describes as 'an inheritance that can never perish, spoil or fade' (1 Pet. 1:4). Christians are called to live now in the light of that future – that is what it means to 'store up for ourselves treasures in heaven'. This is one of many places in the Bible where we are urged to live with the eternal perspective that we considered in Chapter 1. We are to make sure that our priorities in life are focused on things that last for ever. Of course we have to spend a great deal of our time engaged in the essential business of this world – earning a living, buying and preparing food, and much else besides. But our heart is to be elsewhere. We are to be those who know that this world is not all there is – our eyes are to be fixed on heaven.

What is it in this world that will endure for ever? Only people – those who trust in the Lord Jesus Christ. The Egyptian pharaohs were buried in pyramids surrounded by their most precious possessions, presumably in the hope that they would be able to enjoy their treasures in the next world. But that is not possible – as an old Italian proverb puts it, 'The last coat a man wears has no pockets in it.' All we can take with us beyond death is ourselves. That means that our personal holiness must be at the top of our priorities. Our growth into the likeness of Christ is the one thing that we will be able to keep when we enter God's new creation. We cannot take our car, clothes and house; but our faith, hope and love will remain.

For a number of years I spent most of my time working with students. Sadly, some of those I remember as keen Christians during their time at university are no longer living the Christian life; others are far less committed than they used to be. In almost every case, this turning from Christ has been caused either by a relationship with a non-Christian or by over-commitment to work. Of course Christians should work hard and earn the wages that they are paid, but some people do far more than is necessary. It may be that we are more likely to be promoted if we are the last to leave the office every evening, but there are some things that are more important than promotion. If the cost of the longer hours is that we have no time or energy left to read the Bible and pray, or to meet with other believers, then it cannot be worth it. In the light of eternity it is surely better to have a worse job and be holy than to have a better one and be worldly. That may mean that we are less well off.

So what? Does it really matter that we drive a Mini rather than a Mercedes, live in Hackney not Hampstead, and go on holiday in Skegness instead of the Seychelles?

If holiness is one priority, evangelism must be another. Nothing we do is more significant in the light of eternity. We should be concerned, not just about our own relationship with Christ, but about the spiritual health of others as well. That will have implications for our use of time. Take parents, for example. They have an important responsibility to raise their children to know and love Christ. What is more important – that children each have a room of their own, a large garden and the latest toys to play with, or that they grow up knowing and loving the Lord Jesus? Some parents spend so much time earning money to improve their family's standard of living that they have little time left for the raising and nurture of their children, which they largely delegate to others.

And what about our money? Do we store up treasures on earth or in heaven in our use of it? Surely our comfort in this world should be a far lower priority than giving others a chance to enjoy a place in the next? Does the way we spend our money reflect that? John Laing is a great example. At a young age he was earning a good salary in the family construction business. He bought a modest house on an estate, in which he lived for the rest of his life. He worked out that he could provide for his family quite comfortably on only a third of his income. He saved half of what remained and gave the rest away to gospel causes. After a while the income from his savings provided more than enough to live on, so he gave all that he earned away. When he died in 1979, his personal fortune was just a few hundred pounds. To this day, the money that he left in trust is being used to fund significant Christian ministry.

Could we give more money to help evangelistic work at home and abroad? It is easy to condemn other believers for the extravagance of their lifestyles by pointing to areas of expenditure which we would never consider. 'Fancy spending all that money on school fees and exotic holidays – just think how many missionaries it could have supported.' But is there really no area of needless extravagance in our lives? Are there more sacrifices we could make for the sake of the gospel? That will mean that we do not enjoy all the material comforts that our friends take for granted. No doubt they will think us odd if we do not live up to the materialistic expectations of our age, but, if we look to heaven we will be able to resist the pressure to conform. We are set free from the earth-bound existence of those who live around us because we know that this world is not all there is – we have a guaranteed future.

A generous Father

> *Look at the birds of the air; they do not sow or reap or store away in barns, and yet your heavenly Father feeds them. Are you not much more valuable than they?* (v. 26)

Someone might say, 'It is all very well pointing to a great future to look forward to, but what about now? We are not in heaven yet, and for the time being we have to be concerned about earthly matters such as food and clothing. How does our future hope of heaven help us to pay the mortgage, put food on the table and buy shoes for the kids?' The answer is that God does not simply provide for us in the future. He is our generous Father who richly provides for us in the present. His loving care of us should remove any anxiety about such things. We are to trust him and not to worry. That is the main point of Jesus' teaching in verses 25 to 34. The word 'worry' appears six times. The general point is found right at the start of the section: 'Therefore … do not worry about your life, what you will eat or drink; or about your body, what you will wear' (v. 25).

The 'therefore' links what Jesus says here with his teaching in the previous section. Materialism does not pay or satisfy, so we would be wise to make sure that our lives are not focused on attaining material possessions. But such worry is not simply foolish; it is also needless. Since God has provided us with the greater gift of life itself, will he not also provide us with the lesser gifts of food and clothing, which are necessary to sustain that life (v. 25)? And if he gives the birds all the food they need, can we not trust him to do the same for us who are infinitely more precious in his sight than they (v. 26)? So why worry? It is unnecessary and it does not achieve anything anyway (v. 27). And think of wild flowers in a field. Their beautiful colours produce a rich tapestry which makes the finest clothes of even the wealthiest people look drab by comparison (vv. 28–29). God put them there. If he is prepared to go to all that effort to adorn a field, how much more will he be concerned to clothe his own children (v. 30)? Jesus concludes, 'So do not worry, saying, "What shall we eat?" or "What shall we drink?" or "What shall we wear?" For the pagans run after all these things, and your heavenly Father knows that you need them' (vv. 31–32).

We must not misunderstand what Jesus is saying. This is not a warrant for laziness. God's provision does not appear independently of human effort. The 'lilies of the field' may not 'labour or spin', but the implication is that we humans must, if we are to be clothed. We will have to put time and effort into gaining the necessities of life. But, as we do so, we are freed from a sense of anxiety about such matters, knowing that ultimately their provision does not depend on us but on our loving, generous, heavenly Father. Nor is there any excuse here for complacency. We cannot absolve ourselves of responsibility for the starving in the world on the grounds that it is God's job to meet their needs. He gives more than enough food to provide for everyone on earth. We are to blame if we are too selfish to distribute it fairly.

Jesus is very clear that he expects us to be distinct from non-believers in our attitude to food and clothing. Non-believers 'run after' such things but we, by contrast, are 'to seek first God's kingdom' (v. 33). Are we doing that? The goal of the advertising industry is to create dissatisfaction within us – to convince us that we want, and even need, something that we do not yet have. How easy it is to be seduced by that message. Our longings become directed towards things in this world as we gaze at the catalogue or the television screen. 'If only I could have that dress, that wine, that meal...' But we are to entrust such things to God. He will give us what we really need. That knowledge sets us free to concentrate on the eternal – God's reign in our lives, as we submit to Christ, and his reign in the lives of others, as they hear and believe the gospel.

Contentment

If we live in the light of those two great realities – our guaranteed future and our generous Father – we will stand out as being thoroughly distinct from those around us. In a culture that always wants more, we will be marked by our contentment. One author has concluded his book on Christian behaviour in a consumer culture with a chapter entitled, 'The shocking impact of a contented Christian'. He argues that consistent disciples will be more obviously different from the world in this area than perhaps any other.

> In an age in which the whole direction of people's lives is dominated by climbing the career ladder, acquisition of material goods and never being satisfied, for a Christian to be able to honestly say, 'I am fine as I am, I don't need anything' is a tremendous and glorious shock to the non-Christian's system. It is the cutting edge. To be known as an able colleague and yet to have no greater ambition than to be content in God, is so astonishing, it makes people sit up.[7]

Will we store up for ourselves treasures on earth or in heaven? Will we serve God or money? If our sights are set firmly on the invisible God and his eternal kingdom, we will be released from anxiety concerning the visible and temporary — we will be content.

Discussion questions

1. How and why has the great ambition of many in our society changed in recent years?
2. How does materialism 'tether our hearts to the earth'?
3. Why is it that materialism does not pay or satisfy?
4. How can we store up treasures in heaven?
5. How can Christians strike a balance – meeting their legitimate needs in this world without falling prey to the temptations of materialism?

For personal reflection

Are you content? If not, why not? And what steps might you take to achieve that contentment?

Notes

1. Gudrun Kretschmann, *10 Keys to Prosperity* (Thorsons, 1994).
2. Mark Fisher, *The Instant Millionaire* (Simon and Schuster, 1996).
3. John R.W. Stott, *Christian Counter-Culture* (IVP, 1978), 155.
4. *The Times*, 8–4–99.
5. *The Sunday Times*, 18–10–98.
6. *The Daily Telegraph*, 24–11–97.
7. John Benton, *Christians in a Consumer Culture* (Christian Focus Publications, 1999), 152.

4

Purity in a World Obsessed with Sex

For this reason a man will leave his father and mother and be united to his wife, and they will become one flesh. (Gen. 2:24)

It is God's will that you should be sanctified: that you should avoid sexual immorality; that each of you should learn to control his own body in a way that is holy and honourable, not in passionate lust like the heathen, who do not know God. (1 Thess. 4:3–5)

'Sexual intercourse began in nineteen sixty-three, between the end of the Chatterley ban and the Beatles' first LP.' Those are the words of Philip Larkin in his poem 'Annus Mirabilis'.[1] My fairly basic knowledge of biology tells me that that is something of an exaggeration, but undoubtedly something did happen in the 1960s which resulted in a revolution in how society views sex. It was not long ago that sex was the great taboo. Those were the days when the 'Carry On' films were considered risqué. They seem very tame and dated now. Sex does not blush any more. It is 'in your face' – the 'nudge, nudge, wink, wink' era is gone.

'If it feels good, do it'

We have moved a long way from the prudish attitudes of a previous generation. As far as many are concerned, the Bible's teaching on the subject of sex belongs in the past. It is dismissed as being hopelessly out of date, a relic from a bygone age. The old morality made some sense when the threat of disease and unwanted pregnancy was great and when there was no reliable safeguard against them. But the great medical discoveries of the twentieth century have changed all that. Penicillin has eradicated syphilis and the pill provides a cheap and reliable form of contraception. Even if contraception fails, new techniques have made abortion both safe and effective. So there is nothing to stop us from giving full expression to our sexual urges: 'If it feels good, do it'. The teaching of Sigmund Freud strengthened that appeal. The repression of sexual desire was not just unnecessary; it was positively dangerous – leading to all sorts of psychological problems in later life.

All of these different factors combined to produce a powerful argument which won the day. The 'Permissive Society' was born. It led to dramatic changes in our country's sexual behaviour. More people began having sex with more partners at a younger age. In 1965, 33 per cent of eighteen-year-old boys and 17 per cent of girls of the same age had had sex. That represented a significant increase on the figures from the decade before, but by 1977 the numbers had risen dramatically again – to 69 per cent and 55 per cent. They have continued to rise since, but more slowly. By 1994, only one per cent of British men and four per cent of women were virgins on their wedding day.[2] It is clear that the Bible's teaching has been rejected by our society. That will make it very hard for us to live God's way, especially if we cannot understand why God should restrict sex to marriage and suspect that he is just a killjoy. As we consider the Bible's teaching on sex, I hope we will see that it makes sense – God's instructions are for our good. But I want to begin with a brief look at our culture's view of sex.

'Just a bodily appetite'

A superficial survey might suggest that our society has a high view of sex. It is everywhere – on the television screen, in our magazines, on the advertisement billboards. We are obsessed with it to such an extent that C.S. Lewis could say, 'Sex is rapidly becoming the one thing venerated in a world without veneration'.[3] But a closer look reveals a very low view of sex. For many, it is little more than a bodily appetite. 'If you are hungry, have a Mars bar; if you are thirsty, have a Coke; if you are turned on, have sex.' The other person is almost incidental. Sex is about me, satisfying my desires, my appetite, improving my performance – it is the 'Playboy, Playgirl' philosophy. One writer has expressed it well. Commenting on the effects of the sexual revolution in the 1960s, he says,

> It has led not merely to a change in sexual mores, but to a change in the concept of sex. People no longer make love; instead they "have sex". Reduced to a bodily appetite, desire is emancipated from morality and placed on display in the supermarket of pleasure. Sexual desire then ceases to be focused on the other person … and becomes centred instead on bodily sensations.[4]

Sex, then, is seen simply as a natural urge that must be satisfied – on a par with eating and drinking. The only moral imperative left is, 'wear a condom'. A recent sex education leaflet said it all: 'Any kind of sex is good sex as long as it is safe sex'. That is not to say that everyone is promiscuous – far from it. There are those, at one extreme, who make casual sex a way of life. Wilt Chamberlain, the American basketball star, claims to have slept with twenty thousand women. But most people do not approve of such behaviour. Many do have standards concerning their sexual activity, but they would not dream of imposing them on others. Ours is a tolerant, permissive culture. It simply says, 'It's up to you.' 'If you want to keep sex within certain boundaries, that's fine, and if you want to sleep around, that's fine too – it's your choice.' Anything goes, as long as it is safe. Here is how one university's safe sex leaflet put it: 'Enough of this moralising. Sleep with whoever you can, whenever you can, but do it carefully.'[5]

What does the Bible teach?

1. Sex is a precious gift of God

If a superficial view of our culture suggests that it has a high view of sex, we find the opposite among Christians. We have managed to give the impression that God is against sex. In some Christian circles the great heroes are virgins – the implication being that there is something inherently sinful about sex. No doubt it is such negative teaching that led to the behaviour of one Victorian bride who reputedly drugged herself on her wedding night and left a note for her new husband which simply said, 'Do your worst.' That is very sad. There is nothing in the Bible that supports such a warped view of sexuality. God is not a prude who is embarrassed about bodies and their functions – he made our bodies and he made

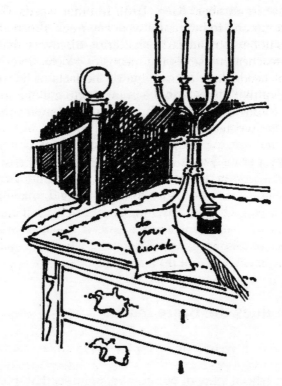

us sexual beings. Sex is a precious gift from the Creator. One whole book of the Bible, the Song of Songs, is a eulogy to the wonder of sexual love. Even the apostle Paul, dismissed by many as a repressed bachelor, taught that sex was good. He encouraged married couples to have sex frequently (1 Cor. 7:3–5).

2. Sex is the means of procreation

In Genesis chapter 1, the creation of male and female is followed immediately by these words: 'Be fruitful and increase in number' (Gen. 1:28). In other words, God's first command to humanity was 'Have sex! Procreate!'

It is not exactly an earth-shattering discovery that the Bible teaches that sex is the means of procreation – you do not need much knowledge of the facts of life to be aware of that. But it is still a point worth making in our culture. One contributor to a survey of women's magazines has written:

> Turn to the pages of *Elle* or *Marie Claire*, and children, along with decisions about having children, are absent.… In one recent issue of *Cosmopolitan* a long supplement on "Sex and your body at 20, 30, and 40" did not mention childbirth once – which is odd, given that pregnancy and childbirth affect the female body and the average female sex life more profoundly than any other experience in those three decades.[6]

Those magazines are full of sex, so I am told, but there is no mention of children. Many people today do not link sex and childbirth. Contraceptives have broken that connection in people's minds. And, if contraceptives do not work, there is always the morning-after pill or a quick abortion.

I am aware that I am on sensitive ground at this point, but do not let anyone tell you that having an abortion has no more moral significance than having your tonsils out. It is far more serious than that. The destruction of human life should never be taken lightly but, tragically, it is – day after day in this country. It may be that you have already had an abortion. If so, remember that God is merciful and will forgive us, no matter what we have done, if we turn from our sin and trust in Jesus. Abortion is wrong, and it carries its consequences like every other sin, but there is forgiveness in Christ.

Sex is, at least in part, about producing children – that is how the Creator designed it. But we must not stop there. There has been a long tradition in Christian ethical teaching, from the days of Augustine and Aquinas, focusing on what is called 'natural law' – it is still prominent in Roman Catholic thinking today. It looks for the natural function of sex and concludes that it is designed for procreation. Morality is then derived from that purpose, so a sexual act that does not permit the possibility of procreation is deemed to be immoral. That is the foundation of the Roman Catholic ban on contraception. It is true that sex is designed by God for reproduction, and the Bible expects that a married couple will want to have children. But that is not the only purpose of sex, as we will see in the next section.

3. Sex expresses and strengthens love and commitment

Throughout Genesis chapter 1 we read that everything God made was 'good' (Gen. 1:4,10,18,21,25,31). But, in Genesis 2, for the first time we find something that is not good. God says, 'It is not good for the man to be alone' (Gen. 2:18). What Adam is lacking is not sexual fulfilment, but relationship, not orgasms, but company. So God creates the woman – Eve. Adam is delighted by what he sees – she is the perfect partner for him. Theirs is a match truly made in heaven. The writer then says, 'For this reason a man will leave his father and mother and they will become one flesh' (Gen. 2:24). Those words are foundational for the Bible's understanding of sex and marriage. Both the Lord Jesus and the apostle Paul quote them in the New Testament.

According to the Bible, sex is not just about me – my appetite and my desires; it is about relationship. It has been designed by God to be the pleasurable means by which two people express their total commitment and love to one another. They are not limited to words or even flowers – they can say it with their bodies. We understand the concept of body language. A handshake is an expression of friendship. A kiss may say something more – it can signify affection. Sex is the most extreme form of body language. A couple is naked and completely exposed before one another, and in their sexual union they are saying, 'I love you and I am completely committed to you for life' – at least that is what God intended to be communicated by sex. The result, in the words of Genesis, is that two people become 'one flesh', which speaks of more than just their physical union. It refers to the deep union that exists at every level of their lives. The act of sex is designed both to express that bond between a couple and to establish and strengthen it. It operates as a kind of glue that binds a couple together.

So, sex is not simply a release of tension or the satisfaction of a bodily urge. It is far more profound than that. No matter how casually people may go about it, there is no such thing as 'casual sex' – that is a contradiction in terms. Paul makes that point in his first letter to the Corinthian church. Some Christians at Corinth had been visiting prostitutes and had thought nothing of it. But Paul takes them back to God's teaching in the book of Genesis: 'Do you not know that he who unites himself with a prostitute is one with her in body? For it is said, "The two will become one flesh"' (1 Cor. 6:16). Paul is not teaching that the act of sex produces a *de facto* marriage – that is not the argument. He is simply reminding the Corinthians of the purpose of sex and therefore of the seriousness of what is going on when a couple has intercourse. There can be nothing casual about it. One writer has put it well: 'Nobody can really do what the prostitute and her customer try. Nobody can go to bed with someone and leave his soul parked outside.'[7]

A columnist in *Elle* celebrated her ideal relationship as follows:

> It was to be the perfect sexual release. The only ring that bound us had ribbed latex attached to it. It bound us till death – till I was bored to death. The idea had been to meet once, maybe twice a month, tops. And there'd be none of that waiting by the phone stuff.[8]

Compare that with God's view of sex – I know which I prefer. One writer concluded her survey of women's magazines with these words:

> This then, could be the fate of the modern reader of women's magazines: aspiring to freedom and sex, she ends up simply alone and lonely. So do her male partners. Is this then, what women really want?[9]

It is not just the 'casual fling' that is ruled out as a result of the relational nature of sex as designed by God. This is also the reason why Christians condemn pornography. For pornography depersonalizes those who are photographed – reducing them to mere objects for another's gratification. It dehumanizes the viewer as well. The dignified human, made in the image of God, becomes little more than an animal, driven by lust. This is becoming an increasing problem as pornography becomes more and more available, especially on the internet. In a recent survey, 60 per cent of young men and 20 per cent of women admitted to having downloaded sexual images. Thirty-three per cent of men and 23 per cent of women had had sexual chats on-line.[10]

What about masturbation? Given that sex is about relationship, it follows that this practice is a departure from that ideal – it is not using sex appropriately. Having said that, it is worth noting that the subject is never referred to in Scripture, which, at the very least, should tell us that the teaching of a previous generation that masturbation is a great evil was overstated. We should not allow this area to become the barometer by which we judge the health of our Christian lives – that is to let it get way out of proportion. But we should remember the strong words of Jesus concerning our thought life. He taught that whenever we look at a person lustfully we are committing adultery with them in our heart (Mt. 6:28).

4. Sex is for marriage

For this reason a man will leave his father and mother and be united to his wife, and they will become one flesh. (Gen. 2:24)

It is because the Bible teaches that sex leads to two people becoming one flesh that it insists that its proper context is within marriage. If sex is the body language of lifelong commitment, then the expression of that is only appropriate when the commitment has been made. If I have sex without that commitment, then I am saying something with my body that I am not saying with my life – it is a form of lying. Sex is only permitted within marriage. So what does the Bible understand by marriage? Genesis 2:24 is, once more, foundational. It is the text from which the rest of the Bible's teaching on the subject is expounded.

Marriage is heterosexual

When God provided a helper and companion for Adam, he created a woman, not another man. They were designed to complement one another. That fact immediately precedes the first reference to marriage in the Bible. It was 'for this reason', the writer of Genesis tells us, that 'a man will leave his father and mother and be united to his wife'. In other words, God established marriage to be the context in which our complementary sexuality is expressed. It is to be between a man and a woman – not between two people of the same sex. Marriage is heterosexual and sex is only for marriage, so there is no context in which homosexual sex is right.[11]

Our society considers the idea that homosexuality is sinful to be an intolerant and narrow-minded view. How can it be wrong if it is natural for some people? But what comes naturally to us is not always right. A child may have an inbuilt desire to hit anyone who upsets him, but most people would accept that he should be urged to repress that desire. Our human nature has been flawed in every area as a result of our sinfulness. That is equally true of everyone – we all have warped sexual desires. So there is no room for a judgemental attitude. We should show love and compassion towards those who battle with homosexual temptation.

Perhaps that is a personal battle for you. If so, remember that God has promised not to test you beyond what you can bear – you do not have to give in to your temptations (1 Cor. 10:13). It may help to talk with a trusted Christian friend. Many people experience these feelings only for a period in their lives – they may go away. But if they do not, God will give you the strength to resist them if you look to him. And whatever you do, do not give in to the rhetoric of the gay lobby as it urges you to 'come out' and accept who you are. Our identity as Christians is in Christ, not in our sexuality. The great reality that defines who we are is not our sexual desires but our relationship to the Lord Jesus – we are children of God.

Marriage is exclusive

The writer of Genesis says, 'The man will leave his father and mother'. That does not mean that he must break off all contact with his parents as soon as he gets married. The assumption is that, before marriage, his main social unit was the family of his birth. But, at marriage, a new social unit is established – he 'leaves' his parents and is 'united to his wife'. From now on, his main loyalty is to her; and the wife's main loyalty is to her husband. The leaving of parents makes it clear that a new state of affairs has begun. It is a decisive step – it tells the world that this relationship is not just a friendship; it is a new, exclusive social unit – a marriage. In a context in which everyone lives in the family home until they get married, the leaving of one home and the setting up of another is declaration enough that a marriage has taken place.

Our society is very different. Most people leave home long before they get married. The mere act of moving in with someone does not express a commitment to a life-long exclusive relationship. Different societies mark that commitment in different ways. The means does not matter – what is important is that the new state of affairs is marked in a public way so that everyone knows that a new exclusive relationship has begun. In our culture that means a marriage ceremony. It is only after this public commitment to one another that the couple is to have a sexual relationship. That is clear from the order given in Genesis. A couple's 'leaving' precedes their 'uniting', which is followed by their becoming 'one flesh'.

Once again, this teaching is very different from the attitudes of most people in our society. We have seen already that many divorce sex from relationship altogether, let alone an exclusive relationship. The harmful effects of that separation are increasingly recognized. We fool ourselves if we pretend that 'there is nothing in it'. Many non-Christians would agree. According to one survey, only 20 per cent of Oxbridge students think that one-night stands are acceptable. The rest feel that sex should be kept within a loving relationship.[12] But that need not mean marriage, for 'It's OK as long as we love each other' is the common view. But what is meant by love?

The group Wet, Wet, Wet had a hit with their song 'Love is all Around' from the film *Four Weddings and a Funeral*. The song contains this striking line: 'You know I love you, I always will; my mind's made up by the way that I feel'. Surely the first half of that lyric is cancelled by the second half? How can I be sure that you will always love me if your mind is made up by your feelings? Feelings come and go. As a friend of mine has put it, 'If you want to show someone that you really love them, don't take them to bed – take them up the aisle. If you're not prepared to do that, don't have sex with them, because the chances are they will only get hurt'.[13] The sexual revolution has left many wounded, insecure individuals in its wake. Sex is very powerful. When a couple has sex it is not just their bodies that are involved. Their whole personality and emotions are affected. A bond is being created with a glue that is designed to bind them together permanently. So it is not surprising that it hurts when a sexual relationship breaks up. It is difficult enough to break up when there has been no sex involved, but having had a sexual relationship makes it even harder. Many people have been hurt, feeling as if they have been used and then discarded. Some are nervous of ever really committing themselves to anyone else again. If they engage in sexual activity, they try hard not to let their emotions get involved, which demeans God's gift of sex almost to the level of prostitution.

That still leaves cohabitation. When a couple decides to live together they are making a big commitment – surely sex is permitted in that context? But, once again, the answer is no – not because God is a spoilsport, but because he knows what is good for us. Ian Stuart Gregory has defined cohabitation as:

- A type of compromise relationship designed by a man by which he can both have sex with a woman and get her to do his ironing without any commitment in return.
- A psychological state in a woman in which she deludes herself into believing that marriage is more likely if they live together first.
- A trial marriage which turns out to be a trial and not a marriage.[14]

They are cynical words, but there is much truth in them. Cohabitation demands much, but offers no security. It is easy for one partner to leave the relationship and the resulting pain can be as great as that experienced in a divorce. 'But surely', say some, 'it is better to make any mistakes before the commitment of marriage. That avoids the messiness of divorce later. It must be sensible to check that we are compatible.' But the reality is that those who cohabit before marriage are 50 per cent more likely to get divorced within five years of marriage than those who have not lived together first. It is possible to find out a great deal about someone without living with him or her. Someone says, 'But we still need to check that we are sexually compatible.' What does that mean? Unless there is some serious medical problem, a man and a woman will be physically compatible. That does not mean that they will enjoy perfect sex from day one, but the best context in which to work out any sexual difficulties is not within the insecurity of an impermanent relationship – but rather within the covenant of marriage. Ultimately, marriage depends not on compatibility but on commitment.

Marriage is lifelong

In Matthew 19:6 Jesus quotes Genesis 2:24 and then adds, 'So they are no longer two, but one. Therefore what God has joined together, let man not separate.' Marriage is for life. When a couple marries, God is involved – whether or not they get married in church. They are not simply making a human contract with each other; God has joined them together into 'one flesh'. That unity is not to be broken – God hates divorce. He allowed it in the Old Testament period as a concession because of human sin, but he never likes it. It is not permitted for the Christian except when there has been 'marital unfaithfulness' or desertion by an unbelieving partner (Mt. 19:9; 1 Cor. 7:15), and even in those cases it is far from clear that remarriage is allowed.

There are those who reject marriage as an outdated institution, but most still believe in it. People love to get *Hello* magazine and look at the pictures of the latest celebrity wedding. The majority of young people still hope to get married some day. But always, in the back of their minds, is the assumption that if things do not work out, they could always get a divorce. Forty per cent of engaged couples do not expect their marriages to last.[15] Their fears are likely to be realized – more than one in three marriages in Britain do end in divorce. The cost to society is enormous – once again God's way is proved to be best. For example, £400 million is spent on legal aid in divorce cases every year. That is nothing compared to the human cost both to adults and their children.

Many decide to bail out of marriages if they are not going well, but that is not an option for the Christian. Those who are thinking of marriage would be wise not to rush into it. A lifelong marriage will need more than hormones to sustain it. The Puritans of the seventeenth century had the right attitude. Their approach in choosing a spouse was to look, 'not necessarily for one whom one does love here and now ... but for one whom one *can* love with steady affection on a permanent basis'.[16]

Perhaps you are conscious of having failed already – you are separated or divorced. Be reassured – neither divorce nor remarriage is an unforgivable sin; but they are sins nonetheless. Christians who have fallen in this area can still be full members of the church, in some cases after appropriate discipline, but they will need to recognize that what has happened was wrong and a departure from God's will.

Marriage is not for all

It is clear from the Bible that although marriage is the norm, singleness is good and is not second best. The Lord Jesus never married and never had sex, and yet he was the most perfectly whole human being who ever lived. The apostle Paul urged others to stay single so that they could share the opportunity he enjoyed for undivided devotion to the Lord Jesus and his service (1 Cor. 7:34). It is true that it is not good for us to be alone, but our need for companionship can be met by friendships rather than marriage.

Some choose to remain single, others would love to be married. Either way, we should accept our current state in life as a gift of God. We may not remain single all our lives, but we should rejoice in the benefits of the single state while we have it, rather than lament its disadvantages. And if you are single and tempted to feel sorry for yourself for being 'left on the shelf', remember that God does not have a shelf. Paul wrote to the Christians at Corinth: 'I promised you to one husband, to Christ, so that I might present you as a pure virgin to him' (2 Cor. 11:2). If we are Christians, we can be confident that Christ has chosen us as 'his bride' and we will remain married to him for ever.

The call to be different

It is God's will that you should be sanctified: that you should avoid sexual immorality; that each of you should learn to control his own body in a way that is holy and honourable, not in passionate lust like the heathen, who do not know God. (1 Thess. 4:3–5)

We have seen that the world has a very different understanding of sex from that of the Bible. Once again, we Christians are called to be distinctive in our behaviour. We are not to follow the way of 'passionate lust'. Each one of us who has read this chapter will need to repent in one way or another. We all fall short of God's standards whether in thought, word or deed. For some the struggle is in the whole area of thought life. For others the challenge is something that you are doing physically which you know is wrong – whether on a casual basis or with a particular person. If we are left asking, 'How far can I go?' then we are asking the wrong question. God calls on us not to sail as close to the wind as we can, but rather to take efforts to pursue what is good. We are to control our bodies 'in a way that is holy and honourable'. Each of us will need to think what practical steps we should take to enable us to do that more effectively.

It is a high standard and we have all failed. There may well be things that we have done of which we are deeply ashamed. If so, let us remember the good news of the gospel. Jesus did not just die for certain sins. If we have trusted in him, we have been forgiven for all that we have done wrong and are perfect in God's sight. Paul wrote these stern words to the Corinthians: 'Neither the sexually immoral nor idolaters nor adulterers nor male prostitutes nor homosexual offenders ... will inherit the kingdom of God.' But then he added, 'And that is what some of you were. But you were washed, you were sanctified, you were justified in the name of the Lord Jesus Christ and by the Spirit of our God' (1 Cor. 6:9–11). We are new people in Christ; now we must look to him to give us strength to live a new life.

Discussion questions

1. How have society's attitudes towards sex changed over the past decades? What are the results?
2. Compare and contrast the views of the world with the Bible's teachings on sex as:
   A precious gift of God
   A means of procreation
   An expression of love and commitment

3. What does the Bible understand by marriage? How does sex fit into that relationship?

For personal reflection

How do you fall short of God's standards for purity in thought, word or deed? Once we have identified these things and repented of them, what is the good news in Christ (1 Cor. 6:9–11)?

Notes

[1] Philip Larkin, *High Windows* (Faber Paperbacks, 1979), 34.

[2] Mike Starkey, *God, Sex and Generation X* (SPCK, 1997), 47.

[3] C.S. Lewis, *God in the Dock* (Fount, 1979), 18.

[4] Roger Scruton in *The Times*, 15–6–97.

[5] Quoted in the UCCF 'Relationships Revolution' material.

[6] Social Affairs Unit Survey', quoted in *The Sunday Times*, Nov. 1997.

[7] Lewis Smedes, *Sex in the Real World* (Lion, 1979), 124.

[8] Quoted in *The Sunday Times*, Nov. 1997.

[9] 'Social Affairs Unit Survey'.

[10] *The Times*, 9–10–98.

[11] See Thomas E. Schmidt's *Straight and Narrow* (IVP, 1995) for an excellent treatment of the subject.

[12] Cherwell and Varsity Survey, Nov. 1995.

[13] Ian Garrett in a talk to students at Durham University.

[14] Ian Stuart Gregory, *No Sex Please, We're Single* (Kingsway, 1997), 99.

[15] Nick Pollard, *Why Do They Do That?* (Lion, 1998), 47.

[16] J.I. Packer, *Among God's Giants* (Kingsway, 1991), 347–48.

5

Certainty in a World in which Everything is Relative

'I am the way and the truth and the life. No-one comes to the Father except through me.' (John 14:6)

A sparrow's flight

One of my set texts for A-level history was *A History of the English Church and People*, written in the early eighth century by Bede, who lived in Jarrow in the north east of England. If I am honest, my heart sank at the thought of having to plough my way through it. I could not imagine that three hundred pages of Anglo-Saxon history, written by an obscure monk, could possibly be interesting. But they were – I was gripped.

Many of the stories still stick in my mind nearly two decades later. One that stands out above all is the remarkable account of the conversion of the kingdom of Northumbria to the Christian faith in 627. King Edwin's wife became a Christian and he was on the brink of following her, but first he felt it right to convene a meeting of his chief advisers to discuss the matter. A number rose to speak in turn, including one unnamed nobleman who delivered a speech of powerful eloquence:

> Your majesty, when we compare the present life of man on earth with that time of which we have no knowledge, it seems to me like the swift flight of a single sparrow through the banqueting-hall where you are sitting at dinner on a winter's day with your thanes and counsellors. In the midst there is a comforting fire to warm the hall; outside, the storms of winter rain or snow are raging. This sparrow flies swiftly in through one door of the hall, and out through another. While he is inside, he is safe from the winter storms; but after a few moments of comfort, he vanishes from sight into the wintry world from which he came. Even so, man appears on earth for a little while; but of what went before this life or of what follows, we know nothing.[1]

It is a striking illustration of the human predicament. We must live our lives within the confines of a closed universe. It is as if we are trapped within a single room. We can study all the details of that room intently, but we cannot look outside. As a result, our knowledge is severely limited. Even if we were to discover everything possible about the world in which we live, we would still be very ignorant. We fool ourselves if we think that our experience encompasses all that exists. Individuals, and indeed humanity as a whole, appear on the canvas of eternity as briefly as a sparrow, as it flies through a room. We can know nothing of the wintry world outside.

Is there anything out there?

Imagine that a group of people was born in one locked room and lived all their lives within it. These people have frequent discussions about the world outside. One day the argument gets more heated than usual. Anthony starts it all off. He tells the group that he has been studying the room for years and is at last ready to publish his findings. Careful investigation of the contents has revealed an intricate design. Could that washing machine, for example, with its five different cycles, really have come into existence by chance? Does it not rather point to someone, or something, outside the room who made it and put it there? But, he has to acknowledge, no one has ever seen anything except what exists inside – so it is possible that there is nothing else. We just cannot know.

By this stage Bernard is very frustrated and cannot hold it in any longer. 'There you go – nailing your colours to the fence again. Stop being so woolly! The trouble is that you are blind to reality. We can be absolutely certain that there is something out there. My mother brought me up to believe that the world outside is inhabited by big giants and little pygmies, and I have never had any reason to doubt it. The truth is that the giants put our ancestors in here years ago and have kept us locked up ever since, but the pygmies are determined to release us, and one day they will.' Bridget protests immediately. 'You've got it all wrong', she says. 'You speak about "the truth"; let me tell you what it is. There are no pygmies, just giants – loads of them. And they are not our enemies – they don't even know we are here. But they will do when the great earthquake happens and opens a hole in the wall so that we can be free.' Beatrice laughs loudly. She cannot disguise her contempt for such primitive faith. 'Grow up, you two', she says. 'Why can't you face reality and recognize that there is nothing out there – there never has been and never will be.' That is when the dispute really gets going.

Maurice listens for a while and then loses patience. 'Calm down! There's truth in what you are all saying. I have to say I prefer to think of it rather differently. I like to think there is something out there. In fact, only yesterday I shut my eyes and tried to picture what it might be and a very clear image came into my mind. I saw green people with white spots on their foreheads. The way I see it, they aren't giants – I don't like the thought of them at all – far too intimidating. No, they are our size, if not a little smaller; and very friendly – that's what I like to believe. But if you want to see things differently, that's fine – lets all be tolerant of one another and stop this awful bigotry.'

What are we to make of those different points of view? How can Bernard and Bridget be certain that their beliefs correspond to reality? And how can Beatrice know that there is nothing outside? They are all making dogmatic statements about something of which they cannot be sure. Maurice may be eccentric, but at least he is more humble. He acknowledges that his is not the only way of looking at the question. But only Anthony is being entirely reasonable. He sticks with the facts and refuses to go further. For those who have spent all their lives in a single room, any statement about the outside cannot be more than guesswork.

Can we know the truth about God?

Let us suppose for a moment that that room represents time and space. The question under discussion is whether or not there is anything outside those observable realities: 'Is there a God?' and, if so, 'What is he like?' Anthony represents the agnostic. He recognizes that his mind can only take him so far. If he uses the word 'truth', it is to speak of those things within the material world that can be proved by strict scientific method. Anything else belongs to the realm of speculation. He is prepared to recognize that there may be something 'out there' but, then again, there may not be.

Bernard, Bridget and Beatrice are the believers. They all hold to different faiths. Yes, Beatrice is a believer as well. Her faith is atheism – the dogmatic belief that there is no God. All three of them are becoming increasingly unpopular in today's world. They speak of 'truth' as an objective, exclusive fact. They are certain that they are right and those who disagree with them are wrong. But surely they should have more humility and less arrogance? Truth is not an appropriate word to use when speaking about a world which is outside our experience; at best we are simply guessing.

That leaves Maurice, the mystic. His religion fits very comfortably into the modern world. He notices that most of those who call themselves agnostics are atheists in practice – they live as if there is nothing outside this world of time and space. He is not happy with that. He feels the need for some 'spirituality' – something to give him a sense of direction and purpose. So he adopts a religion or philosophy that suits him, choosing on the basis of intuition, feelings and personal preference. It is very likely that he will not take one of the traditional religions off the peg; he will design his own, drawing on a variety of different sources. He may still speak of 'truth', but if he does it refers to what is 'true for me', recognizing that others may have a very different 'truth'.

'Relativism' is a jargon word that few people understand, but you do not need to understand it to live by it. Whether they know it or not, most people in our society are relativists. Relativism rests on the assumption that absolute truth does not exist, or, if it does, we can never discover it with certainty. We are trapped in the material world and can do nothing but guess about what lies beyond – whether it concerns belief in God or ultimate morality. So, truth becomes a flimsy concept that is entirely subjective. The boys of Boyzone summed up what many believe in a recent song: 'No matter what they tell you; no matter what they say; no matter what they teach you; what you believe is true.' The same idea is expressed in the title of one of the Manic Street Preachers' albums: 'This is my truth, tell me yours'. The theologian Don Cupitt has made the point with characteristic vigour: 'Capital "T" truth is dead … Truth is plural, socially conditioned and perpetually changing.'[2]

'The man from outside'

Let us return to the discussions in Northumbria in 627. A speaker has just likened our lives to the brief flight of a sparrow through a hall in winter: 'of what went before this life or of what follows, we know nothing'. We are limited to what we can see in the brief span of our existence on earth. But the speaker did not stop there. He continued, 'If this new teaching [Christianity] has brought any more certain knowledge, it seems only right that we should follow it'.[3] He speaks good sense. There is no virtue in being ignorant when that is not necessary.

Those who are trapped inside a single room all their lives cannot by themselves discover the truth about what lies outside, if there is anything there at all. But what if someone from outside came to visit them? Then they would have 'certain knowledge' – they would know the truth. That is the great claim of Christianity. Coifi, the high priest of Northumbrian paganism, was the final speaker at the meeting before King Edwin.

He exclaimed: "I have long realized that there is nothing in our way of worship; for the more diligently I sought after truth in our religion, the less I found. I now publicly confess that this teaching clearly reveals truths that will afford us the blessings of life, salvation, and eternal happiness."[4]

His speech won the day and the whole kingdom converted to Christianity. There is one key word in Coifi's speech: 'reveals'.

Christianity claims to be unique among the religions of the world. All other religions are attempts by human beings to reach after God. They begin in the closed room of human existence and, as a result, they cannot be more than speculation. But Christianity begins not on earth, but in heaven; not with humanity, but with God. He has taken the initiative to make himself known. Jesus is 'the man from outside' who can tell us with authority what we could never have discovered for ourselves. He is not bound by the world of space and time. He is the eternal Word of God.

John's Gospel begins with this great declaration: 'In the beginning was the Word, and the Word was with God, and the Word was God. He was with God from the beginning' (Jn. 1:1–2). But then, at one moment in history, he entered our world: 'The Word became flesh and made his dwelling among us' (Jn. 1:14). Now, at last, it is possible to know the truth about God. It is not discovered by the power of human reason or mystical experience, but through revelation. 'No-one has ever seen God, but God the One and Only, who is at the Father's side, has made him known' (Jn. 1:18).[5] Jesus himself said: 'I am the way, the truth and the life. No-one comes to the Father except through me' (Jn. 14:6). Other religions such as Islam also claim to be revelation from God, but there is no solid evidence to back up their claims. Christianity, on the other hand, is based on real history. Christ proved himself to be the Son of God by his perfect life, his teaching and, above all, by his resurrection from the dead.

'Your word is truth'

Jesus did not remain on earth for long – after the resurrection he returned to his Father in heaven. But, despite his absence, we still have access to truth. God has not simply revealed his truth in the person of his Son. We also find his revelation in the words of the Bible. Jesus made it clear that he accepted the Old Testament as the word of God. On many occasions he quoted it with authority. For example, when questioned about his views on divorce, he referred to a verse we looked at in the previous chapter – Genesis 2:24. Those are the words of the narrator of Genesis, and yet Jesus introduces them in a remarkable way: 'Haven't you read … that at the beginning the Creator "made them male and female", and said, "For this reason a man will leave his father and mother and be united to his wife …"' (Mt. 19:4–5). Did you notice that Jesus equates the words of the human writer of Genesis with the words of God? It is, according to Jesus, 'the Creator' who is speaking there. The Bible is indeed a human book. It was written by about forty different authors, and their books bear the marks of their different styles, personalities and historical contexts. And yet, the Bible is also a divine book. God ensured by his Holy Spirit that the human authors wrote exactly what he wanted them to write. The Old Testament is the word of God – that was the conviction of Jesus.

Jesus accepted the Old Testament as God's word and he also prepared for the New Testament to be God's word. He chose apostles 'that they might be with him and that he might send them out to preach' (Mk. 3:14). He spent a great deal of time with them so that they knew what he taught and could pass it on to others when he had gone. But how can we be sure that they accurately recorded the words of Jesus in the New Testament? We can be sure because Jesus did not leave them on their own after he had ascended to heaven.

Shortly before his death, Jesus comforted his disciples with the promise that when he had left them he would send 'another Counsellor' – someone who would be alongside them as he had been. The Counsellor's identity is soon revealed – he is 'the Spirit of truth' (Jn. 14:17). Jesus continues, 'the Counsellor, the Holy Spirit, whom the Father will send in my name, will teach you all things and will remind you of everything I have said to you' (14:26). That is not a promise for all believers of all time – how can Jesus remind us of what he has said to us when he has never spoken to us directly? He is speaking to those who were with him during his earthly ministry and, in effect, he is saying: 'When I am gone, the Spirit will come to you and make sure that you do not forget what I have taught you, so that when you record it and pass it on to others, you will get it right.'

That is why we can trust the New Testament – it is not based on fallible human recollection but rather on the Holy Spirit of God. Jesus did not simply remind the apostles of what they had been taught previously; he also promised that the Spirit would reveal new truth to them. 'I have much more to say to you, more than you can now bear. But when he, the Spirit of truth, comes, he will guide you into all truth' (Jn. 16:12–13). Once again, that promise was fulfilled in the teaching of the apostles, preserved for us in the New Testament. It contains some truths which they could not have understood before the resurrection of Jesus and which were revealed to them subsequently by the Spirit. So the whole Bible, both Old and New Testaments, is revelation from God, the one who cannot lie. As Jesus himself said to his Father, 'your word is truth' (Jn. 17:17).

As Christians we have received revelation from God – we have the truth. That conviction places us in immediate conflict with our relativist world. In a book called *The Myth of Christian Uniqueness*, Gordon Kaufman has argued that all religions are simply 'creations of the human imagination'. As a result, Christianity should give up any claim to be the exclusive and final truth and recognize itself as 'a human imaginative response to the necessity to find orientation for life in a particular historical situation'.[6] Another writer has added, 'The idea that Christianity … has a monopoly on religious truth is an outrageous and absurd religious chauvinism'.[7] Of course she would be right, if the Christian faith is indeed simply the 'creation of human imagination'. It would be very arrogant to place my guess about the meaning of life above those of others and insist that it alone is true. That would be the equivalent of Bernard, one of the inhabitants of the enclosed room, insisting that the world outside is inhabited by pygmies and giants and refusing to listen to any alternative view. How can he be so sure? But Christians are not like Bernard.

Our knowledge of the truth does not depend on our imagination within the enclosed world of time and space, but rather on the revelation of the one who is from outside – God himself. It is that conviction which compels us to assert that, when there is a clash between Christianity and some other religion or philosophy, Christianity is right and the other is wrong. Our certainty is not arrogance – quite the opposite. It would be a terrible arrogance that said, 'I know God says one thing, but I believe another.' We are called to submit with humility to God's word, even if that clashes with what others believe. For the rest of the chapter we will consider four other imperatives which flow from that fact that we have received the truth.

1. Know the truth

Like newborn babies, crave pure spiritual milk, so that by it you may grow up in your salvation. (1 Pet. 2:2)

Thinking is out; feelings are what matters. For too long, it is argued, the left side of the brain, with its cold logic, has been allowed to dominate. Now it is the turn of the right side, where imagination and the emotions reign. That cultural shift has affected the Christian world. 'Knowledge' and 'doctrine' are increasingly neglected concepts. When we go to church we seek a direct experiential encounter with God and find it hard to see how our minds fit into that. We are tired after a busy week, so we do not want the mental effort of listening to a sermon. Time devoted to the study of Scripture is squeezed out by the greater demand for extended periods of singing. If this trend continues, the results will be disastrous for our spiritual health. Unless we are fed by the 'milk' of the word of God, we will remain stunted in our growth. The truth of God is essential for healthy spiritual life. Without it, we cannot come to faith in the first place, or please God (for his word tells us how to live), or have any true experience of him.

That last point demands expansion, as it is so significant in our contemporary context. Both truth and experience are vital – no one is arguing for just one or the other. But we need to be clear that truth must have priority. It is the truth of God that leads to an authentic experience of God. Our existentialist world asserts that experience carries its own authority – it is considered heresy to argue with it. This has affected Christians to the degree that many now say that the basis of our unity is our common experience. 'Doctrine divides, experience unites – we must unite with all Christians who claim to have had a similar experience of God to ours, despite the sometimes significant doctrinal differences between us.' It is not a great step from there to unite with those of other faiths on the basis of their testimonies to the experience of God in their lives. That is something biblical Christians cannot do. Only those who have responded in faith to the gospel of Christ have a true knowledge of God. Truth, not experience, must come first.

Authentic experience of God flows from knowledge of the truth, which has been uniquely revealed to us through Christ. So if I want to know God in the first place, and then grow in that knowledge, I must begin by learning more about him and what he has done as I study the Bible. To many, that sounds like an excessively dry and cerebral approach to Christianity. It is clear that those who feel that way have not really understood the nature of God's truth. If I really believe what the Bible teaches, it is bound to stir my emotions. It points to a saviour who loved me enough to die for me, and who offers his forgiveness and friendship. I, a guilty rebel, can be called a 'son of the living God'! I would have to be very cold-blooded indeed not to get excited by that. There is nothing cold and unemotional about the life of faith. There are times when we can hardly contain the joy within us, and we want to express that joy with all our hearts. Some will do so with old hymns and liturgical formulae. Others prefer modern choruses, dancing and arms in the air. It does not matter, as long as both are based on the same source: a true knowledge of God the Father, through God the Son, by faith in the word of God given through the Spirit.

God has graciously made his truth known to us in Christ and has preserved that revelation in Scripture. If we want to know him, and then grow in our knowledge of him, we must take the trouble to get to know that truth. There is no substitute for disciplined study of the Bible. Am I going to a church that makes Bible teaching a priority in all its meetings? Am I making sure that I read the Scriptures regularly myself? When did I last read a book that helped me to understand its message? Have I ever bothered to learn some verses? Bible study may be hard work, but it is richly rewarding. And we are not on our own in our study – if we look to him, the Spirit who inspired the Scriptures will open our eyes to understand their message. Our attitude should be the same as that of the psalmist, who said, 'Oh, how I love your law! I meditate on it all day long' (Ps. 119:97).

But the link between studying the Bible and growth in our knowledge of God is not an automatic one. We must hold the first imperative together with the second.

2. Live the truth

> *Do not merely listen to the word and so deceive yourselves. Do what it says.* (Jas. 1:22)

There is always a danger that our study of the Bible will become simply an intellectual exercise. Our heads bulge as we accumulate more and more knowledge, but that knowledge does not always make the short, but essential, journey to our hearts. We need to remember that, in Paul's words to Titus, 'the knowledge of the truth leads to godliness' (Tit. 1:1) – or at least it should.

We all know the caricature of the Christian who is strong on truth but weak on love. He is quick to condemn the evil behaviour he sees in the world and the false teaching within the church, but he is slow to deal with the plank in his own eye. We conform to that type far too often. We need to remember that our first responsibility is for our own private lives before we contend for the truth in the public realm. As we study the Bible we must ensure that we are applying its teaching to ourselves. Perhaps the most common weakness in our sermons and Bible studies is our failure to do that. We leave the teaching hanging in the air rather than bringing it down to earth and thinking through its implications for daily life. We should always take time to ask these questions: 'What will this mean for my life at work, at home or among my friends?' 'What sins do I need to repent of in the light of this teaching?' 'How should my actions and attitudes change?' And then we should pray for God's help to put into practice what we have learnt.

That will include God's command to us to be humble. Paul told the Philippians: 'In humility consider others better than yourselves' (Phil. 2:3). How easy it is to allow the fact that we have received God's truth to go to our heads. We look down on less well-taught Christians and on non-Christians who know nothing of the gospel. We will always be accused of arrogance if we claim to know the truth in a world that has rejected the concept, but let us make sure that we do not add to the offence by having a superior attitude. There is no excuse for such pride. Our knowledge of the truth depends entirely on the gracious initiative of God.

3. Contend for the truth

> *I felt I had to write and urge you to contend for the faith that was once for all entrusted to the saints.* (Jude 3)

A battle rages in the church and in the world – the battle for the truth. Some Christian students were asked whether they had faced opposition from their teachers as a result of their faith. About 50 per cent had, mostly for their conviction that there is such a thing as truth. One philosophy student received this comment at the bottom of a piece of work: 'Remove the parts of this essay that contain absolute values and you will receive a much better mark'.[8] Relativism reigns – everyone has the right to his or her own opinion, and anyone who dares to say that someone else is wrong will be quickly condemned as intolerant. Some Christians in Oxford found that out when they quietly but firmly protested at the use of a church building for a service celebrating homosexuality. The reaction was extreme. An editorial in a local newspaper commented:

> The idea that any mere human … could have any conception of what God is thinking is surely laughable and arrogant in the extreme…. There is no-one … who is so perfect in themselves that they have the right to go around criticizing the behaviour of other people…. A bit of compassion and tolerance is more appealing than a load of bile and bigotry.[9]

None of us wants to provoke that kind of response – it is much easier just to keep quiet. But we cannot – we must 'contend for the faith that was once for all entrusted to the saints'.

Perhaps that is especially important in our churches. Too often we turn a blind eye as the truth of God is compromised. Denominational leaders are allowed to question fundamental doctrines and basic moral principles without censure. Bible-believing Christians should pray for the strength to stand against such error with courage and humility. And we should support others who do so.

4. Proclaim the truth

> *Therefore go and make disciples of all nations, baptising them in the name of the Father and of the Son and of the Holy Spirit, and teaching them to obey everything I have commanded you. And surely I am with you always, to the very end of the age.* (Mt. 28:19–20)

We are called not simply to the negative resisting of error, but also to the positive proclamation of the gospel. That is a counter-cultural activity. No one minds us believing our own faith, but hackles are raised as soon as we start encouraging others to believe it as well. That is especially unpopular when those who receive our message already follow some other religion.

I found myself one morning at 8 a.m. being interviewed by Sue MacGregor on Radio 4's *Today* programme. It was not a pleasant experience. A furious rabbi shouted at me and accused me of 'spiritual Nazism'. My crime was to support a group of students, including a Jewish believer in Jesus, who had invited some of their Jewish friends to a talk entitled 'Was Jesus the Jewish Messiah?' These students used no pressure whatsoever, and the speaker did not browbeat anyone – he simply gave a measured presentation of the reasons why Christians believe Jesus was indeed the Messiah. That, it seems, was crime enough for the rabbi: 'How dare you Christians seek to win converts from our religion! How arrogant to imply that you are better than us!'

There is, of course, no place for a superior attitude that looks down on others. We must respect all people. But even when we have been sensitive and gracious in our evangelism, we will still find that there is likely to be an angry reaction if we seek to win those from other faiths for Christ. It is tempting to respond to that pressure by limiting our evangelism to the 'christianized' – those who have a church background but have drifted away from church activities. That, in effect, is what most churches have done. Evangelism means inviting those on the fringe of church life to attend an event in our building. We have turned the 'go' of Jesus' Great Commission into a 'come', and we interpret the 'all nations' as 'those like us'. 'Mission' for many churches is limited to supporting an aid agency overseas. That may win the praise of our world, but is it faithful to the command of Christ?

The word 'mission' has a Latin word meaning 'to send' as its root. Our 'mission' is what we have been sent by Jesus to do – namely to 'make disciples of all nations'. We are not engaged in mission unless we are seeking to fulfil that command. Social action alone is an important expression of practical love but, strictly speaking, it is not mission. Evangelism must be restored to its rightful place as our top priority. We have received the truth of Christ and it is our privilege and responsibility to pass it on to others. That will mean 'going' to tell others, both in our country and overseas.

Very few people in Britain are churchgoers. We cannot expect them to come to us to hear the gospel – church is alien and rather frightening territory. We must go to them, reaching them on their home ground. That will require a far more radical strategy for evangelism than we have followed in the past. The traditional church 'guest service' may reach some, but the large majority of Britons will never hear the gospel that way. We must think cross-culturally – no one strategy will effectively reach everyone. What could we do to reach the Asians in our area? The Chinese? The Yuppies? The disaffected youth? The elderly? That could mean planting a church; starting a meeting in a pub or old people's home; making contact by knocking on doors to conduct a survey or offer a Jesus video; running a children's activity club. The possibilities are endless. But programmes and meetings in themselves will achieve little. They must be undergirded by relationships. Jesus did not just speak the truth – he lived it. We are called to do the same, not simply within the cosy context of our church family but also within the world – a relativist world that will not often thank us for our efforts.

We all need to ask ourselves, 'What will "going" mean in practice for me?' Am I spending enough time with non-Christians? Could I live in a different area where there is little or no gospel witness? Should I seek to work overseas? Christ is the truth for all people, the only way to God. They need to hear the good news of Christ whether they live in secular Europe, the Muslim Middle East, Hindu India or Communist China. If I believe the truth, I must proclaim it – whatever the cost. It will not be easy, but there is a great promise to spur us on. Jesus says, 'And surely I am with you always, to the very end of the age.'

Discussion questions

1. Imagine yourself in the locked room. With whom would you have identified most closely before you came to Christ and why: Anthony, Bernard, Bridget, Beatrice or Maurice?
2. How can we as Christians know that we have the truth?

3. What are some specific ways in which you, in your life, can more actively live the truth and contend for the truth?

4. How can we communicate the truth of the gospel to a relativistic world?

For personal reflection
What will it mean for you to 'go' to reach others with the gospel?

Notes

[1] Bede, *A History of the English Church and People II*, (Penguin Books, rev. edn 1968), 127.
[2] Quoted in Pollard, *Why?*, 126–7.
[3] Bede, *History*, 127.
[4] Bede, *History*, 127.
[5] For a brief examination of the evidence that Jesus is God, see Vaughan Roberts' *Turning Points* (OM Publishing, 1999), ch. 4.
[6] Quoted in John R.W. Stott's *The Contemporary Christian* (IVP, 1992), 301.
[7] Rosemary Radford, quoted in Stott, *Christian*, 303.
[8] UCCF Briefing Paper, No. 3.
[9] *The Oxford Student*, 19–11–98.

6

Holiness in a World where Anything Goes[1]

So I say, live by the Spirit, and you will not gratify the desires of the sinful nature. For the sinful nature desires what is contrary to the Spirit, and the Spirit what is contrary to the sinful nature. They are in conflict with each other, so that you do not do what you want. But if you are led by the Spirit, you are not under law.

The acts of the sinful nature are obvious: sexual immorality, impurity and debauchery; idolatry and witchcraft; hatred, discord, jealousy, fits of rage, selfish ambition, dissensions, factions and envy; drunkenness, orgies, and the like. I warn you, as I did before, that those who live like this will not inherit the kingdom of God.

But the fruit of the Spirit is love, joy, peace, patience, kindness, goodness, faithfulness, gentleness and self-control. Against such things there is no law. Those who belong to Christ Jesus have crucified the sinful nature with its passions and desires. Since we live by the Spirit, let us keep in step with the Spirit. Let us not become conceited, provoking and envying each other. (Gal. 5:16–26)

A few years ago, *The Sun* newspaper conducted a survey to find out more about the minds, hearts and integrity of its readers. It claimed to be ecstatic to find out that only 22 per cent would kill a partner for cash and that only 38 per cent would let their wives earn money as a prostitute. 'Congratulations', said *The Sun*, 'we've always known it but now we have the evidence – you *Sun* readers are decent, honest, caring and trustworthy. You're loyal workers, faithful lovers and caring members of the community.' I must confess that when I saw those figures I was not exactly ecstatic – they do not give much cause for exaltation. Perhaps they are exaggerated – *The Sun* is always after a good story, but nonetheless it is clear that the moral health of our nation is not strong.

Young people growing up today often have little, if any, concept of what is right and wrong. It's no wonder that there is so much crime and abortion and an increasing number of teenage pregnancies. As a result, there have been many cries in recent years for something to be done, for a firmer lead to be taken by the government. It was in response to those appeals that John Major launched his 'Back to Basics' campaign at the Conservative party conference in 1993, to the ecstatic cheers of the party faithful. It did not last long. You may remember that it was a dismal failure, partly because some Conservative politicians proved themselves incapable of living up to the standards that were set. But there was a more fundamental problem – just what should the 'basics' be? No one could decide. Our society is increasingly becoming not so much immoral, as amoral. There is little fundamental agreement anymore over what is right and wrong, and that is hardly surprising. The French philosopher Jean-Paul Sartre once said:

> God does not exist and we have to face all the conse-
> quences of this. It is extremely embarrassing that God
> does not exist for there disappears with him all possibil-
> ity of finding values in an intelligible heaven. We find no
> values or commands to turn to.

Dostoevsky, the Russian novelist, summed it up:
'Everything is permissible if God does not exist.' Once
we reject God, it is no longer possible to decide what is
right and what is wrong.

Can we decide between right and wrong?

There was a famous debate in 1948 between two
philosophers – Frederick Copplestone and Bertrand
Russell. Copplestone asked Russell on what basis he differentiated between right and wrong. Russell replied
that he did so on the same basis that he differentiated
between yellow and blue. Copplestone pointed out the
obvious inconsistency there – he said that it is possible
to differentiate between colours on the basis of what one
sees, but one cannot see what is right and wrong, good
and bad. So, how does one distinguish between those
things that cannot be seen? Russell was in a corner, and
in the end he simply said that he did so on the basis of
his feelings, which is a very weak reply. That is all the
atheist can say, and it is a profoundly flimsy basis for
morality. In some cultures people love their neighbours
and in others they eat them – both on the basis of feeling.
Are they equally right? If feelings determine morality,
then how can we stand up against a tyrant like Adolf
Hitler? No doubt, the Holocaust felt right to him.[2] We are
left with the only moral dictum that many people in our
society know: 'If it feels good, do it.' That was the great

watch-cry of the permissive society that was launched in the 1960s. It is still with us today. Released from the shackles of religion and Victorian morality, I am free to believe what I like and behave as I want. It sounds so attractive, and yet, it has brought slavery, not liberation.

In some parts of the country, older people are too scared to leave their homes. Many other people are imprisoned by their own self-destructive behaviour, addiction to drugs, sexual licence and petty crime. Still others are lonely and insecure – victims of divorce and unfaithfulness; they cannot escape from the consequences. Successive governments have seen the problems and have been powerless to do anything about them. So our society continues to spiral out of control towards moral chaos. We live in an amoral world. That is not to say that no one has any standards; it is simply to say that there is no agreed standard any more – 'You're entitled to your own morality, that's fine, just don't go preaching it at me.' We are back to the relativism we considered in the last chapter: 'There's no truth except my truth, no morality except my morality.' That is the climate in which we live as followers of Jesus Christ. In that context, it will be very difficult indeed to affirm that there is right and wrong, let alone to live by those standards.

We are called to be holy in a world where anything goes. 'Holy' is a 'God-word'. It means to be 'set apart'. God is uniquely set apart from everything that he has made. He is set apart supremely by his moral perfection. As those who belong to him, we are called to 'be holy as he is holy' (1 Pet. 1:16) – to reflect his character and perfection in the way that we live our lives. That will not be easy. We are natural conformists, but the Bible calls on us to stand out and be different. No doubt you have been conscious of how hard that will be as you have considered the 'distinctives' in this book. Perhaps you are asking, 'How could I even begin to live like that?' If so, Paul's words in Galatians 5:16–26 will provide some answers. As we look at that passage we will consider three steps we will need to take if we want to be holy in an amoral world.

1. We must recognize our sin

Paul stresses in his letter to the Galatians that, as Christians, we have been set free from the law. We have been liberated from the hopeless attempt to get right with God by obeying all of the law's detailed require-ments – we will never reach him that way. The moral law simply condemns us; it never justifies us. Justification comes by faith in Christ and not by obedience to the law. We can only be accepted by God because Jesus died to take the punishment we deserve. He took our sin and its penalty upon himself and, as a result, we are able to receive his righteousness – God accepts us as if we are perfect. It is a wonderful message. But Paul is aware that some might misunderstand or distort it and conclude that: 'It doesn't matter how I live now. All I have to do is trust in Christ and I can be sure that I am accepted by God. I can carry on doing exactly what I want.' Paul counters that attitude in the last part of his letter. He insists that it does matter how we live. We may not be saved by good works, but we are saved for good works. God expects those who trust in Christ to live a godly life.

That is a profoundly unnatural way for us to live because, despite the fact that the Holy Spirit has entered our lives, we still have a sinful nature. The Bible teaches that by nature each one of us is a dis-obedient rebel against God. Left to ourselves, we continue to turn away from him and disobey his standards. Do we recognize that truth about ourselves? It is so easy to become self-satisfied in the Christian life and think we are doing rather well. It is time we stopped believing the lie and started acknowledging the facts. We have all heard testimonies in church meetings of those who tell us how sinful they were before they came to Christ. The implication is that all that is behind them now – 'once I was so sinful, now I am so smug'; that is how it comes across sometimes. But there is no excuse for smugness – even as Christians we are depraved.

Rotten to the core

A few years ago, there was a strike in New York all summer, which left the problem of what to do with all

the household rubbish. One man came up with an ingenious solution. Every evening he went to his cupboard, in which he had a collection of boxes from Macy's, an up-market department store. He placed his rubbish in one of them and then put it outside the front door. Every night for weeks, the box was stolen. You can imagine the distress of that opportunist thief as he got his bounty home and opened his Macy's box with tremendous excitement, only to find a stinking mass inside. Are we not rather like one of those boxes? The outside looks quite attractive, especially when we have made an effort. We can present a good front to the world so that others think that we are fine, upstanding citizens. At times we even fool ourselves by that exterior and are self-satisfied. We need to remember that we are rotten within – we have sinful natures.

Am I prepared to acknowledge that truth about myself? There is not a sin in the book that I could not commit. Listen to these striking words from G.K. Chesterton's character, Father Brown:

> You may think a crime horrible because you could never commit it. I think it horrible because I could commit it. You think of it as something like an eruption of Vesuvius. But that wouldn't be so terrible as this house catching on fire.[3]

Sin is not just out there in other people; it is rooted deep within my nature. Unless I recognize that, I will smugly carry on as I am without making any effort to change. That is why a recognition of my sin is an essential first step if I am to become more holy, 'distinctive', as Christ calls me to be.

A gruesome list

Paul gives us a gruesome list in verses 19 to 21 of the kind of behaviour that flows from our sinful nature. He begins with warped sexual behaviour: 'sexual immorality, impurity and debauchery'. Which of us can say that we are blameless in that area? Many of us have engaged in sexual behaviour that is forbidden by God. What books, films and magazines do we look at and enjoy? What do we stare at on our computer screens? What jokes do we laugh at? What about our thought lives? We look so respectable on the outside, but I wonder how many of us would welcome careful scrutiny from others in this area of our lives. Paul continues the list with false religion: 'idolatry and witchcraft' (v. 20). Those who were involved with some other religion or the occult before they came to Christ are often tempted to drift back to their old ways. Others experience the pull of idolatry in different ways. I am being idolatrous whenever I cling to a view of God that differs from the Bible's revelation of what he is like – that is to worship a God of my creation.

Paul then includes fractured relationships in his list of sins: 'hatred, discord, jealousy, fits of rage, selfish ambition, dissensions, factions and envy' (vv. 20–21). By nature we are very competitive; we long to get our own way – driven by 'selfish ambition'. We gather together with people who want the same things as we do; 'factions', sadly, are a common feature even of church life. Of course, we justify them – we convince ourselves that we are fighting together for some noble cause. But so often our 'discord', our 'dissensions', stem simply from our pride – we want to come out on top. When others prevail, we are full of 'jealousy', 'envy', even 'fits of rage'. Can we honestly say that there is no hint of such things in our relationships at work, home or church? We are too easily satisfied with ourselves because we do not commit what we think are the really bad sins – we do not steal or commit adultery. But God does not grade sins like that. 'Discord', 'jealousy' and 'selfish ambition' may be less obvious, but they are just as bad as other sins and we are all guilty of them. That only leaves riotous excess: 'drunkenness and orgies' (v. 21). Christians are not immune from such sins. It does not take much for us to sink very low.

That is not a comfortable list to read. Paul is saying that this is the kind of lifestyle our natural selves, our sinful natures, engage in. In some people the effects are very obvious and outrageous; others of us are outwardly more respectable. But let us not fool ourselves – there is something badly wrong. The seeds of these sins lie embedded deep within all of us and we have allowed some of them to grow. The fact that we are Christians does not mean that we do not have sinful natures. We must pay careful attention to the very solemn warning that Paul addresses to the Christians in Galatia: 'I warn you, as I did before, that those who live like this will not inherit the kingdom of God' (v. 21). They are strong words, and we need to realize that, left to ourselves, that is how all of us do live. Sin comes quite naturally to us. We will never get anywhere in the battle for holiness unless we acknowledge that truth about ourselves. We must recognize our sin.

2. We must depend on God's Spirit

It is only once we have recognized the truth about our sin that we will begin to see that holiness is not a self-help programme. We will not be able to live distinctive lives simply by our own efforts. Left to ourselves, we will always go away from God and towards the desires of our sinful natures; we are utterly helpless. We will not be able to grow more like Christ simply by pulling our socks up; it will require a miracle. We are forever being told that we can do it all – 'the power lies within'. Norman Vincent Peale's book, *The Power of Positive Thinking*, has sold over fifteen million copies worldwide. It begins with these words: 'Believe in yourself; have faith in your abilities'.[4] The message is 'You have the power – you can do it!' But that is not true. On our own we are helpless. If we want to become like Christ we must depend on God – he is our only hope.

The fruit of the Spirit

The great news is that God does not leave us on our own to live the Christian life. He has sent his Spirit to live within all those who trust in Christ and he will give us the power we need to go God's way. The Spirit is mentioned seven times in verses 16–26. He is the reason why we need not be trapped in verses 19–21, constantly giving in to the desires of the sinful nature. The Spirit opens up the possibility of another way of life. He longs to produce his fruit within us: 'Love, joy, peace, patience, kindness, goodness, faithfulness, gentleness and self-control'. It is a marvellous list of characteristics – the kind that Jesus exhibited in his earthly life. Paul comments, 'against such things there is no law' (v. 23). As one commentator has put it, 'A vine does not produce fruit by act of parliament. They are the fruits of the vine's own life.'[5] In a similar way, these qualities cannot be produced simply by the command of some law, even God's law. No, they are the fruit of the divine nature that has been implanted within us

– God's Spirit. On our own, we are helpless, but we are not on our own if we are Christians. The Spirit of God has entered our lives to give us the help we need to change.

That is a wonderful truth to hold on to. Sometimes we feel so useless. Perhaps this book has had that effect on you. God has pinpointed areas in your life which will need to change, but you feel powerless to do anything about them – the pressures of the sinful nature within, and the world without, are so strong. Or it may be that you are conscious of failure in the battle against one particular sin. You have resolved to fight it over and over again, but you keep losing the battle and giving in to the temptation. It may even leave you wondering, 'What's the point in even trying to change? I never seem to make any progress.' But what Paul teaches in this passage leaves no room for such a defeatist attitude. God's Spirit is with us – the mighty, powerful presence of God, and he can do all things. He can produce his fruit, even in the most unpromising soil. We can expect real, lasting change in our lives. So let us determine not to rely on ourselves, but to depend on God's Spirit – pleading with him to give us the strength we need to resist the sinful nature and to produce his fruit.

3. We must work hard

If I stopped at the end of the second point and said nothing else, you would be in danger of thinking that your role is entirely passive – that all you have to do is, 'Let go, and let God', as the old saying goes. Or, as an awful modern version puts it, 'Don't wrestle, only nestle'. That is a serious misunderstanding. Paul insists that we have a role to play, which is why he addresses us in verse 16. He pleads with us, 'So I say, live by the Spirit'. He would not bother to say that if we did not have to do anything but could leave it all to the Spirit. We have a choice to make. We can either choose to give into the desires of our sinful nature, or we can determine to go the Spirit's way. There is a great promise for those who do the latter: 'live by the Spirit, and you will not gratify the desires of the sinful nature' (v. 16). In other words, if we live by the Spirit we will be able to resist temptation. But first we must make that decision to go the Spirit's way, and that will not be easy. It is not automatic – it will involve hard work on our part.

There is an urgency about Paul's appeal in verse 16, because verse 17 tells us that we are in a battle: 'For the sinful nature desires what is contrary to the Spirit, and the Spirit what is contrary to the sinful nature. They are in conflict with each other, so that you do not do what you want.' I still remember when I first read that verse. I thought, 'Paul knows me – that's exactly my experience.' I had come to Christ and I knew something of the work of the Spirit in my life, giving me a new desire to please him. And yet, at the same time, my old desires would drag me down and I kept on sinning. I hated sin. Deep down, I longed to be like the Lord Jesus and to go the Spirit's way. But the old sinful nature remained and pulled me to go another way. And when I succumbed to its temptations, I always regretted it. That is what Paul means when he says, 'You do not do what you want'. That battle between our two natures is a daily experience for the Christian. There is a tug-of-war going all the time between our natural self without God (the sinful nature) and our new nature implanted by the Spirit.

Keep in step with the Spirit

How can we ever make progress in this battle? It will not be by doing nothing. We are not to relax and watch the spiritual superman, the Holy Spirit, zoom in while we stand by, like Lois, watching him do all the work. No, it will take effort on our part. In Paul's words, we are to 'live by the Spirit' (v. 16) and to 'keep in step with the Spirit' (v. 25). In other words, we are consciously to co-operate with the Spirit's work in our lives. We are to walk with him; we are to go his way. Every time I am tempted I have a choice to make. I can give in, and go the way of the sinful nature, or I can resist, and go the way of the Spirit. Just think back to the last time you were tempted. Think of the battle going on there. You know what you should have done – the Spirit was prompting you to go God's way. But the sinful nature was urging you to go the other way. The choice is ours. So Paul urges us to make the right choice: 'live by the Spirit'; 'keep in step with the Spirit'.

Paul knows that will take effort, which is why he speaks to us in verses 24 and 25. He is giving us reasons for why we should choose to go the Spirit's way. He reminds us of a truth about ourselves: 'Those who belong to Christ Jesus have crucified the sinful nature with its passions and desires.' He is speaking of something that has happened in the past, at our conversion. When we became Christians, we made a decision to submit to Christ as Lord. We decided to go his way through life, the Spirit's way, and not the way of the sinful nature. In effect, he says, we picked up our sinful nature and nailed it to the cross, saying, 'I've finished with that way of life. I don't want to go that way any more.' The implication is clear. If we have sentenced our sinful nature to death and nailed it to a cross, how can we keep on listening to it and following its promptings? It is totally inconsistent behaviour. Despite having made a clear renunciation of sin when we decided to follow Christ, we continue to go its way. We keep going back to the cross to which we nailed our old nature. It is as if we fondle those sins. We even take them down and play around with them again. Paul is pointing out how inappropriate that is. He is saying to us, 'You've finished with that way of life. Live out the decision that you made at your conversion. Say "no" to your sinful nature, and then say "yes" to the Spirit.' We are new people and, as such, we should decide daily, hourly, to live lives that reflect our decision to follow Christ. 'Since we live by the Spirit, let us keep in step with the Spirit' (v. 25). That is our responsibility, and it is hard work.

The Spirit works as we work

A girl came to a clergyman one day and asked him to cast out a demon of laziness from her. He told her to go and buy an alarm clock. She was upset, but it was a brilliant reply. She was expecting God to do everything for her. But if she was to be delivered from laziness, she would have to work at it too. It is only as we make an effort that we find the supernatural work of God the Spirit coming in to help us. But if we sit back and do nothing, we cannot expect him to cast out all our sin – that is not the way he works.

I was teaching my nephew to play cricket recently – that is a very important part of growing up. We only had my bat, which was far too big for him. He tried valiantly, but he could hardly lift it up, which meant that he missed the ball every time. I then gave the ball to his mother and went over to help him. He picked up the bat and I put my hands over his. I wanted him to get the feel of the ball on the bat (it is a wonderful feeling!), so I did not do all the work for him. I let him move the bat and I just gave him the extra strength that he needed. It is a bit like that with us in the struggle against sin. God will not wield the axe on his own and put sin to death in our lives without any contribution from us. It is only when we determine to do what is right and take up the axe ourselves that God the Spirit gives us the strength to use it. We must be prepared to work hard before we will know the power of the Spirit working for us.

So the question is, are we prepared to go the Spirit's way? Every chapter of this book has left us with a decision to make. We can either follow the sinful nature or the Spirit. The choice is ours. On our own we will never be able to become more like Christ – we are far too sinful. But we are not on our own. God has sent his Spirit to live in our lives. He has the power to change us. But he will not do that automatically – first we must decide to go his way. Are we prepared for the hard work which that involves?

Discussion questions

1. How does the world around us decide what is right and what is wrong?
2. Why is it so difficult for us to recognize our sin?
3. How does Paul, in his letter to the Galatians, describe the depth and breadth of our sinfulness?
4. Can we expect real, lasting change in our lives? If so, how?

For personal reflection
Are you prepared to 'wield the axe and put sin to death' in your life? Where will you begin?

Notes

[1] This chapter is based on a talk given at the Keswick Convention in 1997. It appears in *A Voice in the Wilderness*, David Porter (OM Publishing, 1997).

[2] Ravi Zacharias, *A Shattered Visage: The Real Face of Atheism* (Hodder & Stoughton, 1996), 55.

[3] Quoted in D.A. Carson's *The Gagging of God: Christianity Confronts Pluralism* (Apollos, 1996), 21.

[4] Norman Vincent Peale, *The Power of Positive Thinking* (Cedar, 1990), 1.

[5] S.H. Hooke, quoted in F.F. Bruce's *The Epistle of Paul to the Galatians* (NIGTC; Paternoster, 1982), 255.

Wholeheartedness in a World that Can't Be Bothered

By faith Moses, when he had grown up, refused to be known as the son of Pharaoh's daughter. He chose to be ill-treated along with the people of God rather than to enjoy the pleasures of sin for a short time. He regarded disgrace for the sake of Christ as of greater value than the treasures of Egypt, because he was looking ahead to his reward. (Heb. 11:24–26)

A speaker arrived early for a meeting at a university and used his spare time by looking at the societies' notice board. One particular advertisement caught his eye. It had been placed by 'The Apathy Society' and simply said: 'The Apathy Society will not be meeting this week – it can't be bothered.'

'Stay cool'

Universities around the world used to be full of life and vitality. Campuses were hotbeds of Marxism and revolutionary action. Those were the days when student union meetings were packed. Thousands would take to

the streets to march in support of Campaign for Nuclear Disarmament or against Vietnam – students were known for their activism. They were either active in the service of some great cause or in the search for one; but those days are gone. Dr Jonathan Steinberg, formerly the vice-master of Trinity Hall, Cambridge, has written an article under the heading: 'No risk, no cause, no fun – all they want is a good degree'. He says:

> Not long ago, I asked my lecture audience, if anybody in the room thought that anything that he or she would do in life would make any difference to the way the world functioned? They looked at me with pity. Clearly, I had gone mad.[1]

Students are not unique. Our generation has stopped looking for the big idea that explains life and gives meaning to everything, because the assumption is that there is no such big idea. As we saw in Chapter 5, most people believe that there is no ultimate truth. That conviction has robbed life of its meaning. Dr Peter Atkins of Oxford University believes there is nothing outside the material world. He insists, 'The human race must realise how insignificant it is. We are just a bit of slime on a planet belonging to one sun.'[2] What is the point of life, if that is all we are? Jean-Paul Sartre asked once, 'Now God has gone, what have I got to live for?' It is a good question. One writer has commented, 'The world today is full of sufferers from the wasting disease which Albert Camus focussed as Absurdism ("life is a bad joke"). Everything becomes at once a problem and a bore, because nothing seems worthwhile.'[3] It is no wonder that activism has been replaced by apathy. Without meaning, there is no cause worth living for. That is the world we live in – an apathetic world which scorns enthusiasm of any kind at all; a world in which the great values are to be 'cool', 'chilled', 'mellow'. In such a context it will not be easy to be the wholehearted and distinctive disciples of Jesus Christ that he calls us to be.

Sacrifice

I read a biography of Henry Martyn not long ago.[4] He was a brilliant scholar at Cambridge University – he got the top first in maths, as well as being awarded a university classics prize. A glittering academic career lay ahead of him, but he turned his back on all that. Instead, he got ordained and served a curacy in an unfashionable, evangelical parish. Then, at just twenty-four, he set out for India to be a missionary. It took him nearly a year to get there and, almost as soon as he arrived, his health deteriorated – it was never good. He died just seven years later at the age of thirty-one. During those short seven years he managed to produce translations of the New Testament in Urdu, Arabic and Persian which became the foundation for mission work in that region for years to come. Many were converted subsequently, but only one during Martyn's lifetime. He died when he was not much younger than I am, but he made sure that his short life had counted in the purposes of God.

Sixty years ago, Howard Guiness wrote a little book called *Sacrifice*. In it he poses the following question:

> Where are the young men and women of this generation, who will hold their lives cheap and be faithful, even unto death? Where are those who will lose their lives for Christ's sake, flinging them away for love of Him? Where are those who will live dangerously and be reckless in His service?[5]

I have heard questions like that put in talks many, many times and I have often responded inwardly, 'Lord, I want to go all out for you. I'll go anywhere, I'll do anything for you.' But how quickly the fire in my heart grows cold. That is what happened to the Christians to whom the letter of Hebrews was written. They were probably Jewish converts to Christianity who began well in the faith. But then they were persecuted for following Christ and their zeal gradually wore off. Some, it seemed, were even tempted to go back to their old Jewish ways and abandon Christ altogether. The writer of the letter was horrified. He longed to see them continuing in the faith and living wholeheartedly for Christ. One of the ways in which he encouraged those Christians was by urging them to follow the examples of great men and women of faith in Old Testament times. One such hero is Moses. We, too, have much to learn from his example. He provides a model of wholehearted service.

Moses' choice

In human terms, Moses was a man who had it all. It is true that he came from fairly humble origins, but if he was not born with a silver spoon in his mouth, he was reared with it firmly in place. He was brought up by Pharaoh's daughter, so all the privileges of the Egyptian court were at his disposal – a life of power and luxury lay before him. But he rejected all that. He turned his back on prestige: 'By faith Moses, when he had grown up, refused to be known as the son of Pharaoh's daughter' (v. 24). Great prestige was attached to that position; everyone would have known him. They would have bowed and scraped and done whatever he wanted. Family connections would have guaranteed him a top job for life. But he chose to leave all that behind and identify himself, not with the royal family of perhaps the most powerful nation of the world at that time, but instead with a despised, oppressed tribe of slaves. It all began when he was watching the Hebrews at work one day. Moses saw an Egyptian mistreating one of the Hebrew slaves. He looked around to see if anyone was looking, then he intervened. He got involved in a scrap which ended with him killing the Egyptian. He should not have done it, but this act demonstrated the choice that he had made. From then on he was identified firmly with the people of his birth, the Hebrews. He turned his back on prestige.

And he also turned his back on pleasure. 'He chose to be ill-treated along with the people of God rather than to enjoy the pleasures of sin for a short time' (v. 25). No doubt Egypt offered many sinful pleasures, and in his position Moses could have had the pick of them. A life of luxury was guaranteed. And yet he refused all that and instead chose a life of ill-treatment. If you have read the book of Exodus or seen the film *The Prince of Egypt*, you will know what that meant for him. First he had to endure years of exile in Midian. Then, when he finally came back to his home country and returned to the royal court, he came not as an insider, but as an outsider, and a troublesome one at that. What a contrast! In the old days when he approached the court of the Pharaoh everyone had bowed down and saluted, but now no one knew who he was – he was an unknown nobody. It was a very costly choice that he had made.

Moses turned his back on prosperity as well. 'He regarded disgrace for the sake of Christ as of greater value than the treasures of Egypt' (v.26). There was no richer nation in the world. And as a prince of the realm, Moses had the key to the treasure store. He could have taken whatever he wanted, but he threw the key away. He chose a very different way of life, which involved disgrace. His old friends did not want to know him. No doubt they thought he was mad. He turned his back on the very things that most people spend their lives pursuing: prestige, pleasure, prosperity. Instead he chose to go God's way, leading a nation of slaves who most of the time were profoundly ungrateful for his sacrifice. It meant a life of suffering and hardship – it was quite a choice to make. And we are bound to ask: Why did he make it?

Moses' faith

Two key words explain why Moses made his choice: '*By faith* Moses...' (v. 24). If we want to understand what faith means in this context we need to look to the beginning of Hebrews 11. The writer says, 'Now faith is being sure of what we hope for and certain of what we do not see' (v. 1). Moses had a certain hope for the future and he lived his life in the light of that future, even though he could not see it. That is what faith involves: living now in the light of the future which, by definition, cannot be seen. At first sight it seems that Moses made a very foolish choice. He chose pain instead of pleasure in the present. But he was no masochist, no fool – he did it because he believed what God said about the future. Verse 26 makes that clear. Why did he choose 'disgrace' rather than 'treasures'? Because he was looking into the future – 'he was looking ahead to his reward'. He knew it would be worth it in the long run.

There was once an elderly bachelor who owned a large estate. He had no close relatives and could not decide to whom he should leave it when he died. Then he discovered that a distant relative was still alive and living on the other side of the world. He wrote him a letter and asked, 'Would you come and live on my estate? I will give you a cottage and a basic salary, while you get a feel for how to run the estate, and when I die you will inherit it all.' It was not a straightforward decision for the relative. He had a good life, with a decent income, a pleasant house and plenty of friends. In the short term he stood to lose a great deal – while the old man was still alive his standard of living would be worse than that he was currently enjoying. But in the end he did decide to move to England. It was a wise decision. He had his eyes fixed not on the short-term costs but rather on the far greater long-term benefits of moving. After a few months, the bachelor died and the relative was able to move into the mansion and enjoy all the wealth of the estate.

Moses was like that man. In the short term he seemed to make a very foolish choice, but he knew it was worth it because he was 'looking forward to his reward'. He lived with 'perspective' – living in the present in the light of the future. It is impossible to be sure exactly what Moses believed about the future, but the Old Testament gives us a good idea. He would have known about the promises made to Abraham, his ancestor. God had promised Abraham that his descendants would be greatly blessed and that through them the whole world would be blessed (Gen. 12:1–3). In other words, God's plan of salvation was focused on this particular people, the Hebrews. So Moses, in identifying himself with them rather than with the people of Egypt, was not as foolish as it may at first seem. Yes, they were a bunch of slaves, but Moses knew that God had guaranteed that they would prosper. He believed that promise and lived in the light of it.

In his life, Moses received little of the fulfilment of that promise – 'his reward'. He lived in the light of the future. It has been said that faith is like a telescope. It makes what is far away seem closer. Things we cannot see with the naked eye can be seen with the eye of faith. And right through his adult life, Moses had that eye, the eye of faith, fixed firmly on the future and the blessings that God had promised. He never received that full blessing on earth; he did not enter the land of Canaan which was the Old Testament picture of heaven. Speaking of all the great heroes of the faith he has mentioned in chapter 11, the writer to the Hebrews concludes: 'These were all commended for their faith, yet none of them received what had been promised' (v. 39). Ultimately, what had been promised lay beyond the grave in heaven. So, throughout his life, Moses lived a life of faith. He did not actually know that Jesus was coming, but he believed the gospel promises that would finally be fulfilled in him. That is why he can be described as facing disgrace 'for the sake of Christ' (v. 26). It was worth it. We can be sure that he will receive his reward – he will be with Christ in heaven for eternity. He was no fool.

Our choice

What about us? The writer of Hebrews did not tell his readers about Moses just to give them a history lesson. As good Jews, they would have known all about him already. He is introduced here as an example for his readers to follow. Life got tougher for the Hebrew Christians once they began to follow Christ. They were persecuted for their faith and, no doubt, some of them said, 'What's the point? Why don't we just give up? We'd be better off going back to our old Judaism. That, at least, would stop our suffering.' It seemed to be a straight choice between suffering with Christ or an easier life without him. The writer is using the example of Moses to point out that it is not as simple as that. Rather, the choice is between living for the present and living for the future; between living for what can be seen and enjoyed now and what cannot be seen in the future. Ultimately it is a choice between belief and unbelief, between the kingdom of God and this world.

The same choice that faced those Christians in the first century faces us today. Are we going to be those who live for the present, or for the future? Will we live by faith or by sight? For this world or for the kingdom of God? Those are questions we considered in the first chapter of this book, and they underlie all the other chapters as well. Our answers to these questions will determine the whole direction of our lives – what we end up doing, how we do it and why, our attitudes, our chief decisions. The gospel is primarily a promise about the future. There are some wonderful blessings now, and we praise God for them. But most of the blessings of the kingdom of God are still to come – they are stored up for us in heaven. It will only be at the Second Coming that, at last, we will receive the fullness of our salvation.

Meanwhile, we must wait; we must live by faith, not by sight. We are called to live now in the light of an unseen future. If we do that, then there is no doubt about what our priorities will be. The things of this world, which will not last, will be relatively unimportant to us – the CD players, the cars, the computers, the sporting success, the degrees, the jobs, even our families. No one will ask you in heaven, 'Just remind me, how much did you used to earn?' Or, 'How big was your house?' Such matters will be completely irrelevant.

We looked in Chapter 3 at Jesus' challenge to his followers to ensure that our treasure is in heaven and not on earth. I suggested then that that would mean that our priorities in life are holiness and evangelism. Those are the passions that marked the saints of old, great ones like Henry Martyn. Why are there so few like him today? Could it be because our eyes are not fixed on the future? We have become worldly Christians. We still go to church, we still believe the right things in our heads, we still believe in heaven intellectually, but our actions suggest otherwise. We are more concerned with happiness than holiness, with security than souls. Ours is a laid-back religion that seeks to be served, rather than to serve. We want a church that makes us feel good, rather than one that challenges us. So often we opt for religion that costs us little. 'Sacrifice' is a word that is not often on our lips.

Howard Guiness's book *Sacrifice* was the staple diet of Christians in a previous generation. It is amazing how dated it sounds now. The first chapter is entitled 'Poverty'. Guiness writes about how he went on holiday to Switzerland one year and wished afterwards that he had not gone. He could have had just as much relaxation, he says, if he had gone on holiday in this country – and then he could have given the spare money to mission work. He speaks of others who looked through their possessions to see what they could do without. One sold his camera, another his aeroplane. A third cycled all the way to the Keswick convention so that he could save the train fare. Each gave the money gained to the work of the gospel. Guiness writes: 'Money spent on luxuries, little or big, in face of the crying need of the world and the extreme difficulty experienced by mission societies in finding sufficient funds is criminal.'[6] That is strong language. A later chapter in the book is called 'Discipline'. Guiness suggests that we should educate our tastes and appetites in discipline by deliberately eating what we do not like, by finishing our meal while we are still hungry and missing a meal from time to time. He speaks of some students known to him who deliberately slept on the floor with just a sheet over them so that they might get used to hardship, because they knew they were going out to serve Christ in foreign lands. He describes a rugby international who gave up playing rugby for a whole season because he happened to be working with some kids in a youth club. They played soccer rather than rugby and he wanted to get alongside them so he could reach them with the gospel.

I could go on – the book is full of examples like that. It all sounds very old-fashioned. We hear very little these days about the need for sacrifice. Perhaps it was over-the-top – there was a danger of legalism, almost fanaticism but, if we are honest, that is hardly our danger. We go to the opposite extreme. Back in the nineteenth century the Anglican bishop in Sierra Leone had a life expectancy of 18 months – disease was such that most people died a few months after arriving. Yet, there was no shortage of people who went. At one stage Handley Moule, who was the principal of Ridley Hall, a Cambridge theological college, had to plead with some to stay at home because all the best people were going overseas and he was concerned for the state of the church in this country.[7] I do not know many theological college principals who have to do that today. We stress our rights, not our responsibilities; our freedom in Christ, rather than our debt to Christ; our security, rather than our sacrifice. Is it not time that we redressed the balance? Let us think for a moment what Moses gave up.

Prestige

He 'refused to be known as the son of Pharaoh's daughter'. Instead he identified himself with the despised people of God. Prestige is very important in the eyes of the world. We want to be liked and respected. But if we choose to live for the future it is inevitable that our reputation will suffer in the eyes of those around us, who live only for this world. Those who live for an unseen heaven will be seen as 'quaint', at best, and 'mad', at worst. Perhaps you are young and still have career choices to make. Are you prepared to consider the possibility of some kind of paid 'full-time' Christian work at home or overseas? If you are, there are many who will not understand you. When I decided to be a minister, one friend of mine reacted with anger and incredulity – 'That is the end! How could you?' She thought I was throwing my life away. I had been training to be a lawyer, which would have given me a good income and a 'respectable' place in society – what folly to turn my back on that.

It may be that you decide to live and work in a place where the cause of Christ is very weak – perhaps in the inner city in Britain or somewhere overseas. Your friends will think you are crazy. 'Why are you living there? You've got enough money to be able to afford to live in a much nicer place.' I have a friend who trained as a doctor. Everyone approves of that – medicine is a worthy profession. But then he discovered that he was gifted as a Bible teacher, so he gave up medicine to train at Bible college and became a vicar. That made no sense to his non-Christian friends. They were even more bemused when he decided to go to Africa. They would have understood if he had gone to use his medical skills, but in fact he went to teach the Bible. He saw that the great need of people is to hear about Jesus, not to have their bodies healed. He is someone who is very gifted in teaching the Bible. So that is what he chose to do. There is nothing wrong with medicine, but he said, 'If I go as a medical missionary, the needs are so great that no one will give me any time to teach the gospel.' He gave up his medicine. He is living for the future, not the present, and the world thinks he is mad.

I can think of many similar examples. There is one man who is extremely gifted and able as an economist. He was offered a job of national importance in his early thirties, but he turned it down because he was running a young people's group at church. He knew that if he accepted the post he would not have time to continue with his youth work. He said that the most important thing he did in his week was to teach the Bible to those children, so he turned down the salary increase and the top job. That meant missing out on what would have been a great boost to his prestige. He was living for the future, not the present.

Pleasure

Moses 'chose to be ill-treated along with the people of God rather than to enjoy the pleasures of sin for a short time' (v. 25). Are we prepared to say 'no' to pleasure in the short term because our eyes are fixed on the future? So many Christian people do the spiritual splits – they have got one foot in the world and one foot in Christ. They are the most miserable people around – it is very uncomfortable to do the splits. They never really enjoy themselves with their non-Christian friends because they are guilty about much of what they get up to together. They are uncomfortable with their Christian friends as well, because they feel convicted by how spiritually lukewarm they are compared to the others. Are we willing to forgo sin, however painful that might be? In the old days, Christians were not allowed to dance, read novels or go to the cinema. That was extreme and excessively legalistic. But have we not gone to the other extreme? We have a justification for everything now. 'We can't hide in a ghetto – we must live in the real world. It is important that we understand what others are thinking.' So, nothing is off-limits. Just think of the books and magazines you have read and the films and programmes you have seen over the last few months. Many of them have glorified sin. What effect has that had on us? Have we allowed ourselves to be shocked? We are soft on sin. Are we prepared to follow Moses' example and turn away from it?

Prosperity

Moses 'regarded disgrace for the sake of Christ as of greater value than the treasures of Egypt' (v. 26). As Christians, we are often worldly in our attitude to money and possessions, as we saw in Chapter 3. Do I ever stop to ask whether I really need all those savings, all the clothes in the cupboard, the brand new car, the CDs? It has been well said that the real question is not,

'How much of my money will I give to God's work?' We should rather be asking, 'How much of God's money will I keep for myself?' But behind even that question there is a more fundamental one: 'Will I live for this world or the next; the present or the future?'

It so happened that, two days before Henry Martyn died, a portrait of him reached Charles Simeon, the vicar of the church in Cambridge where Martyn had been a curate. Simeon hung it up in his study and he said that those eyes would look down on him and it was as if they said, 'Don't trifle, don't trifle.'[8] That portrait hung in the room where we met to pray when I was at university. It still brought the same challenge. We knew that Martyn had given his whole life to the service of Christ. Would we do the same? He followed in the footsteps of Moses, living wholeheartedly for his master. Together they say to us, 'Don't trifle.' Others may think us very strange if we live for what they consider to be a vague fantasy in the future, but as the old saying goes, 'He is no fool who gives what he cannot keep, to gain what he cannot lose.'

Discussion questions

1. How does Moses' life provide a model of wholehearted service? What was his choice? The character of his faith?
2. Do you know of someone who has lived, or is living, wholeheartedly for Christ – perhaps giving up prestige, pleasure or prosperity? What can we learn from such people?

For personal reflection

Will you hold your life cheap and be faithful, even unto death? Will you lose your life for Christ's sake, flinging it away for love of him? Will you live dangerously and be reckless in his service? What would such commitment look like in your life?

Notes

[1] *The Daily Telegraph*, 26–7–93.
[2] *The Sunday Telegraph*, 7–4–96.
[3] J.I. Packer, *Knowing God* (Hodder, 1973), 27.
[4] D. Bentley-Taylor, *My Love Must Wait* (IVP, 1975).
[5] Howard Guiness, *Sacrifice* (IVF, 4th edn, 1950), 61.
[6] Guiness, *Sacrifice*, 13.
[7] Oliver Barclay, *Whatever Happened to the Jesus Lane Lot?* (IVP, 1977), 39.
[8] Michael Griffiths, *Take My Life* (IVP, 1967), 174.

Battles Christians Face

Vaughan Roberts

The Bible is clear that the Christian's hope and faith are forged in the fiery battles of life. Suffering and temptation shape and strengthen us. But in the twenty-first century many of the crucial difficulties that Christians have always struggled with are lightly treated by some:

- How can I approach feelings of lust in a godly way when 'lust' is now an alluring name for perfume or chocolate?
- How can I battle guilt with integrity when friends encourage me to believe that sin doesn't really exist?
- Why do I feel so depressed when the impression is often given that Christians should always have a smile on their face and in their heart?

In *Battles Christians Face* Vaughan Roberts equips us with practical weapons to face our daily battles with confidence. The teaching in this book restores our hope of living godly lives here and now – lives that honour and bear witness to Jesus Christ.

978-1-85078-728-0

Turning Points

Vaughan Roberts

Is there meaning to life? Is human history a random process going nowhere or is it under control – heading towards a goal, a destination? And what about my life – where do I fit into the grand scheme of things?

These are topical questions in any age, but perhaps particularly so in a largely disillusioned postmodern era such as ours. Vaughan Roberts addresses these questions and others as he looks at what the Bible presents as the 'turning points' in history, from creation to the end of the world.

This book does not read like a normal history book. No mention is made of the great battles and emperors of whom we learnt at school. It will not help you pass exams or score extra marks in a pub quiz. It aims to do something far more important – to help you see history as God sees it, so that you might fit in with his plans for the world.

978-1-85078-336-7

True Worship

Vaughan Roberts

What is the nature of true Christian worship? What are we actually doing when we meet together for 'church' on Sundays? And how does that connect with what we do the rest of the week?

Vaughan Roberts answers these questions and more as he brings readers back to the Bible in order to define what worship is and isn't, what it should and shouldn't be. While we may struggle to define worship by arguing about singing hymns with the organ versus modern songs with guitars and drums, or about the place of certain spiritual gifts, Roberts suggests we are asking the wrong questions. For true worship is more than this – it is to encompass the whole of life. This book challenges us to worship God every day of the week, with all our heart, mind, soul and strength.

978-1-85078-445-6

Exploring Christianity

Missing the Point?

Finding Our Place in the Turning Points of History

Vaughan Roberts

Is there a meaning to life? Where are we going? What is
the purpose of it all?

Christians believe that the answers to all these questions
are found in the Bible. It is an ancient book but it is also
God's message to us today – a message that focuses on
one man, Jesus of Nazareth.

Missing the Point? looks at the most important turning
points of history as outlined in the Bible and considers
where we have come from, where we are going and
what this life is all about.

The Exploring Christianity series looks at some of the
big issues in life, tackles them head on and leads you to
the incomparable person of Jesus.

978-1-85078-763-1

Authentic

We trust you enjoyed reading this book from
Authentic Media Limited. If you want to be informed
of any new titles from this author and other exciting
releases you can sign up to the Authentic Book
Club online:

www.authenticmedia.co.uk/bookclub

Contact us
By Post: Authentic Media Limited
52 Presley Way
Crownhill
Milton Keynes
MK8 0ES

E-mail: info@authenticmedia.co.uk

Follow us: